SAVE OUR LAND
SAVE OUR TOWNS

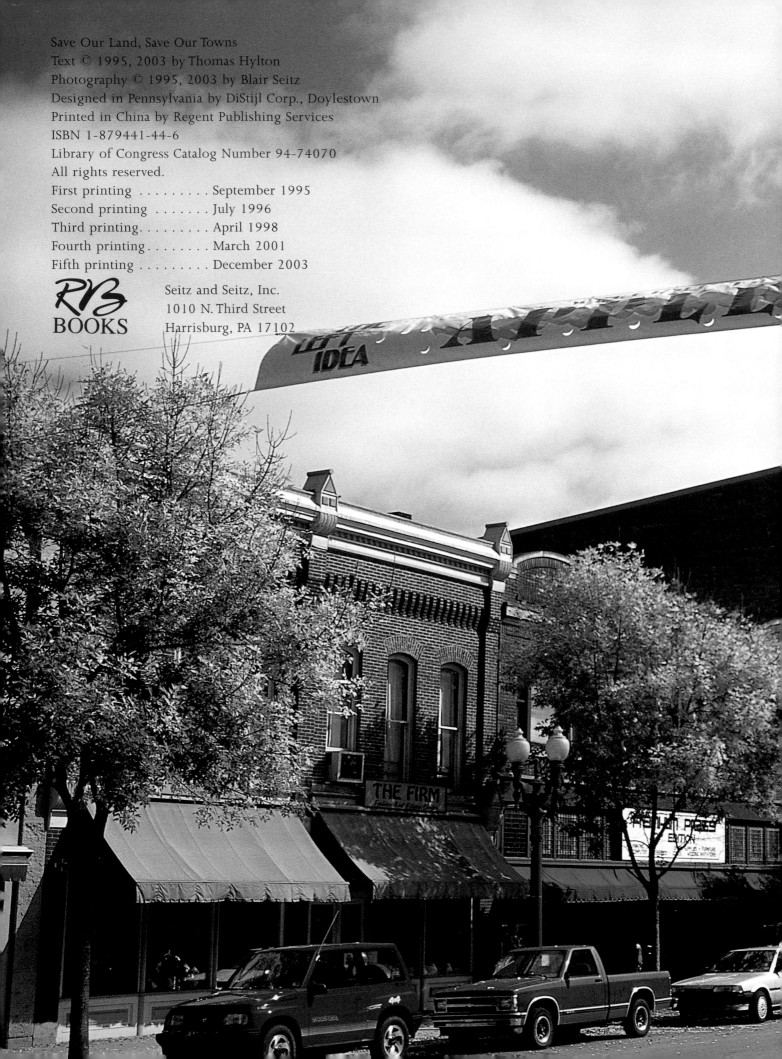

Save Our Land, Save Our Towns
Text © 1995, 2003 by Thomas Hylton
Photography © 1995, 2003 by Blair Seitz
Designed in Pennsylvania by DiStijl Corp., Doylestown
Printed in China by Regent Publishing Services
ISBN 1-879441-44-6
Library of Congress Catalog Number 94-74070
All rights reserved.
First printing . . . . September 1995
Second printing . . . . . . July 1996
Third printing. . . . . April 1998
Fourth printing. . . . . . . March 2001
Fifth printing . . . . December 2003

RB
BOOKS

Seitz and Seitz, Inc.
1010 N. Third Street
Harrisburg, PA 17102

SAVE OUR LAND
SAVE OUR TOWNS

By Thomas Hylton

Photography by Blair Seitz

RB
BOOKS
HARRISBURG, PA

Foreword

Above and previous page: The town of Franklin enjoys a lovely main street.

This is a book about communities, and more specifically about what we can do to preserve and nurture them in Pennsylvania. Since 1982, Preservation Pennsylvania has been helping communities protect, use, and preserve their historic and cultural resources. Sometimes people think of us simply as proponents of old buildings, but our perspective really is much broader than that. It has to be.

Buildings don't exist in isolation. We have to think about the natural and man-made resources and the quality of life that form the context in which buildings do exist. To merit preservation, a historic structure must have a practical use. Its setting must help to tell its story. Thus, to truly have value, a historic structure must be part of a community. So building and maintaining healthy communities is an essential concern of anyone and any organization committed to historic preservation.

Pennsylvania has a rich heritage: It has cities and towns that forged the nation's birth and its great industrial growth. It has fields and farmsteads that have fed our people while forming a landscape that still draws us with its peace and strength. Its communities, both urban and rural, have understood the importance of shared responsibility and interdependence. Without these settings, without this heritage, our historic buildings would have little meaning.

But Pennsylvania is at a turning point. Before us lies the future. Will the Commonwealth build on its heritage, enhancing the lives of our people and making our communities strong, attractive, vibrant places to live, work, and play? Or will it, as some fear, continue the patterns of urban decay, unchecked commercial sprawl, and erosion of the rural landscape?

Preservation Pennsylvania is proud to sponsor Tom Hylton's *Save Our Land, Save Our Towns: A Plan for Pennsylvania*. Building on the Pulitzer Prize-winning editorials he wrote for the *Pottstown Mercury*, Hylton here calls for us to wake up, and look around.

Assess the state of the Commonwealth, he insists.

Demand a new approach to the future, he shouts.

Whether or not you agree that a comprehensive state plan is the answer, after you read through this book, you will no doubt agree that we must save our land, save our towns.

MARY WERNER DeNADAI
President, 1994-1996
Preservation Pennsylvania

We gratefully acknowledge the financial support of the following foundations and organizations in making this book possible: The Berks County Conservancy, The Claneil Foundation, The Glatfelter Insurance Group, The Kinsley Construction Company, The Pennsylvania Department of Agriculture, The Pennsylvania Historical and Museum Commission, The Richard King Mellon Foundation, The Robert R. Anderson Family Fund of the York Foundation, Rosenberger Cold Storage Companies, The Susquehanna Pfaltzgraff Company, The William Penn Foundation, The Wolf Organization Inc., The Wyomissing Foundation, and the York Federal Savings and Loan Foundation.

Table of Contents

PHOTO CREDITS: *All photography by Blair Seitz unless otherwise credited. The author has made every good faith effort to credit and recompense Ernest Frankl for the photo on pages 72-73 but information as to Mr. Frankl's whereabouts was unavailable. The author asks to be contacted by anyone with such information so that proper compensation can be made.*

Shaping Pennsylvania's Future

Successful people and successful corporations set goals and make plans to achieve them. The Commonwealth of Pennsylvania has no plan. In Pennsylvania, government spends billions of tax dollars annually and employs more than 650,000 people without having a clear notion of what it wants to achieve. Individual state agencies attempt to solve problems in their jurisdictions, but they often work at cross-purposes with each other, wasting enormous amounts of time and money in the process.

Here's just one example: The state Department of Agriculture spends millions of dollars annually to preserve farmland by purchasing development rights from farmers. Meanwhile, the state Department of Transportation spends other millions expanding highways into prime agricultural areas, highways that promote the development of that farmland.

What do we really want? Farmland preservation or farmland development?

Here's another example: The state Department of Community and Economic Development spends millions of dollars in attempts to revitalize cities, while, at the same time, the Department of Environmental Protection enforces rules that encourage the development of virgin land instead of older urban areas.

Does Pennsylvania really want to revitalize its cities? You have to wonder.

The lack of a state plan affects all levels of government. Municipalities have an understandable inclination to look out for themselves. Without firm guidelines from the state, most townships seek revenue-producing development and shun anyone too poor to own a car. As a result, the poor are trapped in our cities. That concentration of poverty breeds hatred, crime, and welfare dependency. Meanwhile, the countryside is steadily degraded by the haphazard construction of houses, offices, and stores for people fleeing urban blight.

Pennsylvanians have failed to look at the big picture. We need a coordinated plan to tackle the problems of poverty, crime, deteriorating cities, and environmental degradation.

A state plan is a means of focusing on the future, encouraging us to decide what kind of society we really want. It then coordinates all the agencies and powers of government toward reaching those goals.

We know tomorrow will be dramatically different from today. The question is: Will it be better? A state plan can help assure it is.

Independence Hall, Philadelphia

This is our image of Pennsylvania

We like to think of Pennsylvania as a place of scenic beauty. We buy coffee table books showing Philadelphia's historic houses, the lovely farmland of Lancaster County, the verdant forests of the Allegheny Mountains, the dramatic skyline of Pittsburgh's Golden Triangle.

But have you really looked around you lately? In a growing number of areas, these images are the exception, not the reality! Pennsylvania is being transformed by a short-sighted and pernicious theory of development. It's described in textbooks as Euclidean zoning, but it's more commonly known as suburban sprawl.

Below: A tranquil lake captures the beauty of forested mountains in Little Pine State Park, Lycoming County.

Above left: A farmer harvests alfalfa in Lebanon County. Pennsylvania enjoys some of the most fertile farmland in America.

Above: Handsome houses line a quiet street in Philadelphia's Society Hill.

Pittsburgh's Golden Triangle glows spectacularly in the nighttime sky.

A low-density housing development sprawls across the formerly bucolic hills and valleys of Butler County.

Left: Traffic backs up in Camp Hill, a suburb of Harrisburg.

Below: An abandoned storefront blights the main street of New Castle.

A phalanx of cars fills one of Pennsylvania's omnipresent parking lots, this one at a Chester County shopping mall.

Increasingly, this is the reality

There are no picture books of sprawl. It has already degraded our Commonwealth, and it threatens to rob us of our cities and towns, our farms and forests, of those very things we hold most dear: our sense of place and belonging.

I've had the unique opportunity, thanks to a journalism fellowship, to travel around the United States and Canada to study a new concept in planning that's become known as "smart growth." I've talked to scores of officials and pored over stacks of reports and statistics. I've looked at slums and suburban subdivisions from Miami to Vancouver, B.C.

Planning seems to be a boring, bureaucratic topic. Yet it's the linchpin of our society. You may not see the connections — at first glance or on first consideration — between suburban development and poverty, between zoning laws and the human spirit. But the connections are there, and I'll try to show them to you.

In the next few pages, I'm going to wade through some of the problems we face. Fortunately, there are solutions. Later, I'll get to them and dwell on them. And I'll try to convince you, as I am convinced, that a state plan, based on the principles of smart growth, can lead us out of the suburban wilderness we've wandered in for the past fifty years.

A way of life worth reviving

As recently as the 1940s, the majority of Pennsylvanians lived in neighborhoods of closely spaced dwellings that housed people of varying ages and incomes. Residents could walk to stores, offices, factories, and each other's homes.

My birthplace of Wyomissing, an early 1900s borough just outside Reading, was designed to have all the elements of society in less than a square mile. My family's modest rowhouse was just three blocks from the mansions of the men who founded Wyomissing and owned its industries. It was just two blocks from the Berkshire Knitting Mills, where my father helped develop the world's first nylon stockings. His office was so close he could even walk home for lunch. Our house was near stores, the park, and the Wyomissing Elementary School, where I could walk to kindergarten by myself.

My father's early death left our family in reduced financial circumstances, and we eventually moved to an apartment building in Reading. The city was already declining in the late 1950s, but it was still a wonderful place to grow up in. I could walk to the Fifth and Spring Elementary School and to Northwest Junior High School, where I had a wide range of friends, from the son of a janitor to the daughter of a neurosurgeon.

I could walk to all my friends' houses. I could walk to the Reading Public Library, the downtown department stores, and to choir practice after school at Christ Church. In the summers, I'd check in every day at my mother's office at the Berks County Girl Scouts on North Sixth Street and let her know what I was doing. At least once a week, I'd walk to my grandmother's apartment on North Tenth Street. She was always at home and ready to give me lots of love and attention. And I could be useful. I'd run errands for her at the store and usually have twelve cents left over to buy a Tastykake. I had several adult friends of my own, like Martin Luther Coleman, who ran Sally's Luncheonette and let me read his comic books free.

Later, my family moved to Allentown, another pedestrian-friendly city, where I could walk to William Allen High School and everywhere else I needed to go.

This way of life was inexpensive and fostered a sense of community. Elderly people served as neighborhood watchdogs. Children like me could be independent, but still be observed by adults who knew our parents. Poor and working class people patronized the same schools, stores and public places as the middle class, which helped upward mobility and gave everyone a stake in maintaining public order.

Unfortunately, there is now a whole generation of Pennsylvanians who have no idea what a wonderful and enriching place a city or town can be, especially for a child.

Where did this sense of community go?

What changed?

The nature of our cities and towns. We moved to the suburbs!

Children play in front of Wyomissing's modest rowhouses, located just a few blocks from the mansions of the men who founded its industries.

Reading children walk past a corner store on their way to school. The overwhelming majority of Reading's 13,000 students can walk to school.

Parents chat as students enter Thirteenth and Union Elementary School, one of Reading's many neighborhood schools.

The grandest house in Wyomissing, built by one of its founders, is a short walk from the borough's commercial street, its factories, and homes of every size.

The Costs
of Sprawl

In its early stages, fifty years ago, suburban development was touted as an inexpensive way for people to own a home, enjoy a spacious yard, and avoid the noise and dirt of the city. It started innocently enough. But development soon sprawled out of control.

In the space of just two generations, sprawl has covered over thousands of acres of prime farmland, despoiled once-beautiful landscapes, and chopped up pristine woodlands. It has blighted our surroundings with massive highways and parking lots.

Yet the call of the new suburb is strong and seductive. It continues to lure middle class people and their jobs from cities and towns. Behind they leave shuttered factories, deserted main streets, and decayed neighborhoods. Behind they leave those too poor to finance a similar migration.

Unlike traditional suburbs built through the 1920s, the sprawling nature of postwar suburban development has destroyed our sense of community. We no longer build places that include people of all ages and incomes. We no longer experience the informal meetings and greetings on Main Street that earlier generations took for granted. We don't even have real towns to call home anymore. Instead, we have colorless subdivisions — like Orchard Hills or Fragrant Forests — named for the things that were destroyed when they were built. The names notwithstanding, there is little that's beautiful or inspiring or memorable about them. Yet for decades, that's all we've been building in Pennsylvania.

From Easton to Erie, the trend is the same. Virtually every Pennsylvania city has lost population since the 1950s, usually accompanied by deteriorated neighborhoods and debilitated buildings.

Pittsburgh has hemorrhaged half its people. Johnstown and McKeesport have lost more than half of their residents. Scranton, Wilkes-Barre and New Castle have lost more than a third.

Entire blocks have been wiped out in cities like Erie, which once boasted one of the most vibrant downtowns in Pennsylvania. Altoona is a shadow of its past.

Vacant storefronts and boarded up windows reflect the degradation of a once-proud anchor building in downtown Greensburg. It formerly housed a landmark men's clothing store and a furniture store.

My home city of Reading has lost 27,000 people. Nearly half of Penn Street, its once-thriving main street, has been demolished while surrounding Berks County farmland has been paved over for malls, housing subdivisions, and office parks.

Even our state capital, Harrisburg, has lost 45 percent of its population as people fled the city and spread out their homes, stores, and offices over five surrounding counties.

The flight from cities has even crossed state borders. One of the most pristine areas of Pennsylvania — the Pocono Mountains — has been severely degraded by massive development for people running away from urban problems in New Jersey and New York.

Statewide, thanks in no small part to sprawling development patterns, Pennsylvania has lost more than four million acres of farmland since the 1950s, an area larger than Connecticut and Rhode Island combined.

It didn't have to happen. In states like California and Florida, explosive development since World War II has been fueled by massive population growth. California grew from seven million people in 1940 to thirty-four million in 2000, a 450 percent increase, and Florida skyrocketed from two million residents to sixteen million, an 800 percent increase.

But in Pennsylvania, we've grown barely at all — less than 20 percent in fifty years.

What we've done is spend billions of dollars for new infrastructure to do little more than take our existing population and spread it around. We've ruined our wonderfully livable cities, and ravaged the countryside surrounding them, in order to create a terribly expensive and woefully inefficient way of life. We've tried to run away from urban problems rather than solve them. In the process, we made those problems worse.

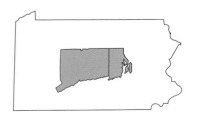

Pennsylvania has lost an area of farmland larger than the combined size of Connecticut and Rhode Island.

CITIES WITH SUBSTANTIAL POPULATION LOSS SINCE 1950:		
Philadelphia	-547,244	27% loss
Pittsburgh	-339,200	50% loss
Scranton	-48,332	39% loss
Harrisburg	-40,141	45% loss
Reading	-27,855	26% loss
Johnstown	-38,817	62% loss
Wilkes-Barre	-33,515	44% loss
McKeesport	-27,183	53% loss
Altoona	-27,321	36% loss
Chester	-28,970	44% loss
Erie	-26,408	20% loss
New Castle	-22,254	46% loss
York	-18,842	33% loss
Williamsport	-14,258	32% loss

Photo © Tom Kelly

New homes in Montgomery County, just west of Philadelphia, sprawl over fields that until recently had been farmed.

Mutually assured destruction

Philadelphia is the first city of Pennsylvania and the birthplace of our nation. It's the perfect example of suburban development's negative effects. As recently as 1950, Philadelphia was a beautiful, safe, and stimulating place to live — one of the most prestigious addresses in the world.

During its first two centuries, a wonderful and efficient system for employing and housing more than two million people evolved in Philadelphia. All the elements of daily life — homes, parks, schools, and workplaces — were contained in more than a hundred neighborhoods, each with its own special identity. People could satisfy most of their needs and wants within a short walk of their homes. An extensive public transportation system could take them anywhere in the city.

Today, Philadelphia is deeply troubled. Although Center City is still thriving, and many vibrant neighborhoods remain, much of the city has been engulfed by urban decay.

About 550,000 people have left Philadelphia since World War II, leaving behind an increasingly poor population. Once known as the "workshop of the world," Philadelphia now has fewer places of employment than its suburbs. The city has lost about 250,000 jobs since 1960.

More than 50,000 once-proud city homes have been abandoned or demolished. Vast areas of north and west Philadelphia are graffiti-covered and falling apart.

Nearly two-thirds of the births in the city are to unwed mothers. Seven of ten public school children come from low income families. Violent crime is an ever-present danger.

As more of Philadelphia's businesses and productive citizens abandon the city, they fuel a vicious downward trend. To compensate for a decreasing tax base, the city has raised taxes and lowered services, which drives away even more businesses and middle class residents.

Meanwhile, the countryside surrounding Philadelphia has been obliterated by housing subdivisions, malls, and office parks built for people fleeing the city.

In just thirty years, the region has lost a third of its productive farmland, even as the region's total population has actually decreased by more than 20,000 residents.

The biggest story of the last fifty years in Pennsylvania, one that should make us ashamed, has been the senseless abandonment of this once-magnificent city, the most historic in America, in order that we could simultaneously destroy some of the most beautiful landscapes and finest farmland in the world.

An abandoned mansion crumbles in west Philadelphia, not far from the Philadelphia Zoo.

Running away from our problems

Typically, the leadership and stability in a community is enhanced by its more educated and affluent citizens. This certainly has been Pennsylvania's tradition. But in Pennsylvania — as in other states, to be sure — postwar suburban development has encouraged the well-off to form separate communities of their own.

Since the 1950s, the poor and minorities have become isolated in our towns and cities, while whites and the affluent have moved to the suburbs and semi-rural areas beyond.

Two of every three African-American babies born in Pennsylvania are born in just four cities: Philadelphia, Pittsburgh, Harrisburg, and Chester. Two of every three Hispanic babies born in Pennsylvania are born in just six cities: Philadelphia, Allentown, Bethlehem, Reading, Lancaster, and York. In the Philadelphia region, 85 percent of the affluent families live in the suburbs while 70 percent of the poor live in the city. Even in prosperous counties such as York, Lancaster, and Lehigh, the pattern is the same: The poor live in the central cities while the affluent live in the suburbs. Statewide, two-thirds of our poor live in our cities and boroughs. The other, much smaller, concentration of Pennsylvania's poor is in our most rural counties, such as Greene, Fayette, and Indiana. Our most suburbanized counties, such as Bucks, Chester, and Montgomery, have the smallest percentages of poor people of all Pennsylvania counties.

This isolation of rich and poor, black and white, is not just morally wrong, it presents a major threat to the future well-being of our Commonwealth. The killing and devastation overseas we read about daily — the Balkans, the Middle East, Africa — all have the same origin: the failure of community. Chronic hatred and conflict and division across the world have occurred because groups of people never learned to respect and live with one another.

In Pennsylvania, as throughout America, the gap between rich and poor is growing. Our minority population is increasing much faster than the white population. Yet many of our whites and affluent are still trying to run away.

Nearly all students are bused to school in Chester County's Owen J. Roberts School District. The student population at Roberts, like that of many suburban school districts, is more than 95 percent white.

The majority of Pennsylvania's black children are isolated in city neighborhoods like Philadelphia's Morton section, at right. Racial segregation deprives all our children, black and white, of the environment they need to learn and grow in a diverse society.

The only house left standing on its block in North Philadelphia displays a mural commemorating a victim of ghetto violence. No child of the Commonwealth should be expected to grow up in an environment like this.

Like many inner city Philadelphia schools, the Taylor Elementary School is covered with graffiti and guarded with razor wire. No child of the Commonwealth should be expected to attend a school that looks like this.

Unprepared, alienated youth

To succeed in the new global economy, Pennsylvania's future labor force must be better educated than ever before. Experts say most people will hold as many as six or seven jobs during their careers. Each of us will need to constantly retool our job skills. Already, there is a large and widening gap between the earnings of high school graduates, which have fallen in real dollars over the last twenty years, and of those who have gone to college.

Unfortunately, huge numbers of our public school children are unprepared for high school, much less college. In Pennsylvania, one in seven children is poor and one in four lives with a single parent. Typically, these children fare poorly in school.

By far, the worst off are our black and Hispanic children, who are isolated in a handful of Pennsylvania cities. Although just 15.5 percent of our public school children are black, two-thirds of these children attend predominately minority schools. Many of these schools are sited in urban wastelands, covered with graffiti and surrounded by trash. Many of their students — often distracted, resentful, and starving for affection — are barely able to master basic reading and writing.

In this milieu, an ominous ghetto culture is evolving, one that purposely rejects traditional American values, warns University of Pennsylvania sociologist Doug Massey. "If whites speak standard American English, succeed in school, work hard at routine jobs, marry and support their children," he writes with Nancy Denton in *American Apartheid*, "then to be 'black' requires one to speak Black English, do poorly in school, denigrate conventional employment, shun marriage, and raise children outside marriage. To do otherwise would be to 'act white'."

For blacks and whites alike, the social trends in Pennsylvania are fearful. Unwed mothers account for a third of all births — triple the rate of thirty years ago — and 270,000 Pennsylvania residents receive welfare. Pennsylvania prisons confine seven times as many inmates as they did in 1970 with little improvement in public safety. Meanwhile, it costs taxpayers $29,500 a year to keep an inmate in jail.

More than 200,000 young people, most of them poor, are enrolled in the Philadelphia School District. There are 90,000 pupils in other city school districts whose student bodies are mostly low income: Pittsburgh, Erie, Harrisburg, Lancaster, York, Reading.

These students will either grow up to be assets to themselves and society or liabilities. Right now, huge numbers of these young people don't even come close to having the attitudes and skills they'll need for productive lives.

To address these problems, some reformers advocate vast increases in school spending to help inner city children. Others call for sweeping reforms in the schools.

Neither will suffice.

Integration is essential

It is unconscionable that some wealthy suburban school districts spend three times as much on their students as the poorest school districts. Every Pennsylvania child is entitled to an equal education. But as long as we have huge concentrations of poor children in any given school, or any given neighborhood, there is little hope for educational equality, no matter how much we spend. These children are overwhelmed by their environment.

My wife has been a teacher for thirty years in the Pottstown School District, which is about 43 percent low-income and 33 percent minority. In the 1970s, she taught in a school near a public housing project. Every fall, she had kids who, at the age of ten, were already burned out, frustrated, and bitter. They had a poor self-image and very little conception of right and wrong. And every year, she witnessed the phenomenon of critical mass. If she had plenty of kids with decent home lives and morals, they would carry the rest of the class with them. She would have order and peace and a productive year for everyone. But if she had too many troubled children, the year would be a disaster.

Considerable research has shown that tracking, grouping students by ability, provides marginal benefits for perhaps the top five percent of our students. But it simultaneously stunts the learning process for everyone else. The vast majority of American children perform best when placed in classes of mixed abilities and backgrounds. Likewise, segregating communities by race and income shortchanges our children and does incalculable harm to our long-term national interest. If we want our children to succeed in sizable numbers, we must have racially and economically integrated schools and communities.

"Urban underclass behavior substantially dissolves with integration into the larger community," writes former Albuquerque Mayor David Rusk in his book, *Cities Without Suburbs*. "Individual poverty and dependency or individual acts of crime certainly do not disappear, but they lack critical mass to blight whole communities... It is the very isolation and hyperconcentration of poor minorities that overwhelms them individually."

We must apply the idea of critical mass — integrating minorities and the poor into the mainstream of Pennsylvania — to foster community, to promote traditional values, and to help all our children become productive citizens. There is no other way.

Left: A teacher's aide reads to an integrated group of children in the Central Dauphin School District, just east of Harrisburg. We need more places where children of all social and ethnic backgrounds can come together.

Below: Fifth graders in the West Mifflin Area School District, just south of Pittsburgh, work on a science project. With a student population that is about 18 percent black, West Mifflin is one of the rare districts in Pennsylvania that mirrors the racial diversity of the state as a whole. Districts like West Mifflin provide the environment needed to give all our children an equal chance to succeed.

Photo © John Heller

One of the many sound barriers that have proliferated along our once-scenic highways.

Left: Once we had Main Street. Now we have commercial strips like this one in Delaware County.

Below: This mall in Montgomery County, like virtually every mall built in America, is marooned by a sea of asphalt.

Photo © Tom Kelly

Is this really the way we want to live?

Let's go out to those suburbs I've railed about and see what's there. Look for yourself.

Once we had towns with vibrant shopping districts and streets bustling with pedestrians. Now we build Wal-Marts, Kmarts and shopping malls. They're invariably massive, windowless, bunker-like buildings, surrounded by huge expanses of treeless blacktop, surrounded by multilane highways.

Our "corporate centers" similarly are huge, featureless buildings, each isolated, each seemingly adrift in a sea of motionless cars.

Our business highways are unrelievedly ugly. They're lined with cheap buildings blazoned with garish signs. These buildings too are set beyond parking lots two or three times their size.

New metropolitan highways are enclosed by sound barriers, Pennsylvania's version of the Berlin Wall. The barriers block any view of the towns and countryside the highways traverse.

This environment is largely the result of a foolish theory that swept professional planning circles in the 1930s. It was implemented with a vengeance after World War II. The new zoning codes required houses to be carefully segregated from factories and offices, which were likewise separated from stores and parks. The narrow streets, small lots, and mixture of stores and homes characteristic of Pennsylvania's traditional villages and towns were outlawed.

Fifty years of such building practices have transformed the Pennsylvania landscape into what Penn State professor Peirce Lewis calls "galactic cities." Masses of housing subdivisions, corporate centers, industrial parks, and shopping malls are scattered as randomly as the stars. This new universe has been designed for cars, rather than people. By rearranging streets and buildings to accommodate the auto, we have devastated the appearance of our towns and countryside.

A car-dominated culture

In accommodating the auto, we have also let it become our only transportation option. This requires that we take our 3,500-pound cars everywhere we go. Bear in mind that while a person takes up only 2 square feet of space, a car hogs 80 to 100 square feet. To provide ample "storage" at each potential destination, we build parking lots. Virtually every building constructed in the last fifty years is bordered, or even surrounded, by a large parking lot.

And these parking lots are empty more often than they are full. Experts estimate that for every vehicle registered in Pennsylvania, we've provided six to seven parking spaces. Because no car is in more than one place at a time, the upshot is this: For every car registered in Pennsylvania — and the total approaches seven million — there are five or six unused parking spaces.

No wonder it is impossible to place buildings in attractive settings. No wonder most trips consist of driving from one parking lot to another. No wonder you can't walk from work to shopping to home. Even when buildings are placed within walking distance of each other, multi-lane highways form impenetrable barriers that make it impossible to go even short distances without getting into a car. Cars are so dominant we rarely build streets with sidewalks anymore. In fact, the state Department of Transportation has banned sidewalks along many of our busiest highways. At many busy intersections, the problem of pedestrian crossing is dealt with simply by prohibiting pedestrians.

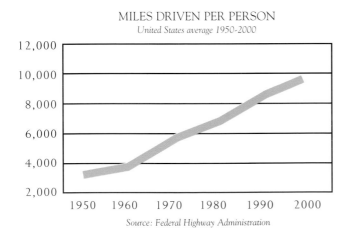

MILES DRIVEN PER PERSON

United States average 1950-2000

Source: Federal Highway Administration

The average single family house generates ten trips a day in the car. The average Pennsylvania worker spends three-quarters of an hour a day just going to and from work, the annual equivalent of a month in the office. Cars are required for trips to the doctor, the store, friends' houses, the park, and everywhere else. You can't buy a loaf of bread without getting into a car to do it.

In the first half of the century, most children walked to neighborhood schools and came home for lunch. Today, children rarely walk anywhere on their own. We don't want them to! They might get run over. So they ride to school on buses, and must be chauffeured everywhere else by their parents. Meanwhile, the elderly

An uneasy pedestrian contemplates crossing DeKalb Pike in King of Prussia, an agglomeration of malls and offices where the car is king and pedestrians are not welcome.

Greatest danger to our life and limb? Car accidents

We are properly fearful of violent crime. But far and away, the greatest cause of unnatural death and serious injury for Americans of all ages — especially young people — is car accidents. *The New York Times* surveyed mortality statistics in the New York metropolitan region and found that a young person growing up in suburban Bergen County, New Jersey, one of the ten wealthiest counties in America, is three times more likely to die before the age of twenty-four than a person growing up in Greenwich Village, Manhattan. The reason? Car accidents.

Car accidents kill more than 40,000 Americans a year. Despite major safety improvements in cars and highways, half of all fatal car accidents are so violent that even seat belts and air bags cannot save the victims. Car fatalities have been part of our society for so long that people tend to take them for granted. Because of the heavy emphasis on crime by the media, most people believe it is the greatest threat to their health and well-being. Statistics tell a different story. It's cars.

dread the loss of their driving privileges, because when that happens, they lose their independence.

Here is one of the unrecognized tragedies of sprawl: In Pennsylvania we have thousands of children who desperately need the love and affection of a responsible adult. We have thousands of elderly people whose lives would be immensely enriched if they could give love and attention to those children on a daily basis. But thanks to our car culture, children rarely enjoy an independent relationship with an elderly person, the very kind I took for granted because I could walk to my grandmother's house.

Life in a small town

For the first five years of their marriage, Dick and Jan Crooker lived the typical southern California lifestyle. They commuted long hours to work and paid thousands of dollars annually to maintain and insure their two cars.

Dick spent three hours a day on the freeway driving to his job at the University of Southern California. Jan, who drove "only" forty miles a day to her teaching job, would delay dinner until 9 so they could eat together. "We felt we were the little squirrels on a wheel," Jan says. "We were working ever harder, running ever faster, but forever staying in the same place. We figured it was no way to live."

They decided to look for a small town where Dick could walk to work and their young son, Adam, could walk to school. Ten years ago, they found their dream in Pennsylvania. The Crookers now own a home on Main Street in Kutztown, just a five-minute walk from Dick's job as a geography professor at Kutztown University.

"It's really convenient to walk to my office whenever I need to," Dick says. "We have most everything we need right here in town. I sometimes go two or three weeks without driving the car."

Jan does "the driving-type things," but her trips are mostly short ones. Their car insurance bill dropped to a tenth of what it was in California. And Jan's grateful she rarely has to play chauffeur for Adam, now fifteen. "As a parent, I think it's important for him to be independent," she says. "He walks or rides his bike to school and baseball practice. He can go to the library or his friends' houses by himself."

Adam recently called from a friend's house where he walked after school. He wanted to go to a pizza parlor instead of coming home for dinner, and then walk to the football game. "I told him to come home first and freshen up, then go," she says. "If we lived in the suburbs, that would have involved at least two or three trips for me, sitting around, hauling kids to pizza parlors, picking them up after football games. And we have friends in the suburbs who do that all the time."

Besides the convenience, the Crookers like the feeling of community that comes with living in a compact town of 6,000 residents. "Little things that happen in this town are big to us," Dick says. "In the suburbs you don't have that feeling of being in a place."

Kutztown University professor Dick Crooker speaks with his students in front of Old Main, just a short walk from the Crookers' home.

On their tenth of an acre lot, the Crookers have a back yard big enough for a patio, a vegetable garden, a dog and two cats. They have a garage with a second floor room Jan uses as her ceramics studio.

"Instead of having this idea you should build a house in suburbia, people should rediscover the great little towns we have in Pennsylvania," Jan says. "When people move out in the country, they love the open air, they love the view, but pretty soon they start complaining about the farmer spreading manure on his field. Soon they want a police department, they want sewers, they want to recreate all the things they left behind.

"It's so much more productive to build on what we already have."

Left: The Crookers can buy most of their daily necessities within a block or two of their home. Kutztown still has a hardware store and many other staples of retailing along its main street.

Below: Dick, Jan and Adam Crooker pose on the patio behind their house. The Crookers' back yard is big enough for gardening, get-togethers, or just sitting out.

Trains have been neglected

Another unrecognized tragedy is that, in our acquiescence to the car, we've largely forsaken the most energy-efficient system of overland transportation known to man: the railroad.

For each gallon of fuel, a train can move a ton of freight three times as far as a truck can, with far more safety and reliability, and with far less air pollution.

A train hauling 140 freight cars requires a crew of just two and moves over a right-of-way no wider than a residential alley. To haul a comparable load by truck requires up to 280 drivers behind the wheel of tractor-trailers covering about five miles of highway.

On one track, a railroad can haul 50,000 passengers in an hour, fair weather or foul. To do the same by highway requires 10,000 cars, each containing four passengers and a driver, traveling over four lanes of highway, in fair weather, and without any accidents. Moreover, once arriving at their destination, the cars must be stored in an area equivalent to sixty-nine football fields, including the end zones.

The Swiss regard railroads as so environmentally superior that they voted in 1994 to gradually transfer all freight passing through Switzerland from trucks to railroad flatbeds. The Swiss have earmarked billions of dollars to upgrade their rail lines, including two new railway tunnels through the Alps for freight.

Europe and Japan are developing vast networks of high-speed rail. They already boast thousands of miles of high-speed lines carrying trains at speeds of 125 to 200 miles per hour. A high-speed rail trip from London to Paris via the new Channel Tunnel, for example, takes about three hours — less than a comparable trip by airplane when travel to and from the airport is factored in.

Pennsylvania was once a world leader in railroad development and technology. At the end of World War II, the Commonwealth boasted an intricate and sophisticated rail system connecting scores of cities, towns, and hamlets.

We threw most of it away.

During the last forty years, as we've spent billions of dollars to pave over the countryside with a network of new highways, we've abandoned 6,000 miles of rail lines in Pennsylvania. Today, only a handful of Pennsylvania's cities and towns enjoy any passenger train service at all. The rest of the state must rely on the auto.

A Swiss train carries tractor-trailers on flatbed cars. The Swiss voted in 1994 to gradually transfer all international truck traffic to railroad flatbeds.

This triple-track railroad bridge over the Susquehanna River, above, has more carrying capacity than ten lanes of nearby Route 81, left, but it takes up far less space.

Pennsylvania's environment degraded

And so it goes. Our dependence on the car spurs the extension of highways and the spread of parking lots and the sprawling of suburbia. In terms of air pollution and environmental degradation and even global warming, no aspect of human life has been more harmful to Pennsylvania's environment in recent decades than sprawling development.

When meadows are stripped, woodlands cut, and wetlands drained in the course of "development," natural ecological cycles are disrupted. The ability of native plant and animal species to survive is severely threatened. It took millions of years for the flora and fauna of Pennsylvania to evolve. During the first 250 years of our Commonwealth's history, they were little disturbed. Yet in recent decades, sprawling development has wiped out eighty species, and it currently threatens nearly thirty others.

The woodlands and wetlands do more than simply protect Pennsylvania's biological diversity. They act as sponges that soak up rainwater, replenishing the groundwater supply and limiting the sediment that flows into our streams and rivers. Development is a double whammy here, for at the same time it diminishes the ecosystem's capacity to recharge the groundwater supply, it places increased demands upon it. Because of their large lawns, shrubs and gardens, and swimming pools, low-density suburbanites use far more water than do their counterparts in cities and towns. In many areas of Pennsylvania, the water table has been lowered by scattered development.

At the same time, the increasing incidence of septic system failure has become a major source of groundwater pollution.

Run-off from sprawling development is yet another problem. It causes flooding. It is the leading catalyst for pollution in our streams and rivers. By means of the Susquehanna River, Pennsylvania controls half the runoff going into the Chesapeake Bay, the largest estuary in the United States. The bay has been declining for more than two decades and faces ecological extinction. According to the Chesapeake Bay Foundation, pollution from uncontrolled development is the bay's worst enemy.

Equally hazardous to Pennsylvania's environment is air pollution generated by cars and trucks.

"We simply can't continue driving everywhere all the time," says Michael Walsh, an air pollution consultant for the American Lung Association. "Sooner or later we have to come to grips with something we don't know how to do. We don't know how to say to people there is a better way to get to work than in an individual car."

Photo © Tom Kelly

Workmen cut a swath through Chester County woodlands for a new four-lane bypass around Exton. The new highway will channel a torrent of sprawling development into pristine Amish and Mennonite farming areas of Chester and Lancaster counties.

Is this a sustainable lifestyle?

But the car population in Pennsylvania continues to increase at a much faster rate than the human population. Our state has far more registered motor vehicles, per person, than any foreign country. On average, Pennsylvania motorists drive thousands more miles annually than the Germans or Japanese, and use three times as much as gas to do it. As long as sprawl continues, the mileage traveled by each Pennsylvanian will continue to mount.

Beyond air pollution caused by cars, there's global warming. Pennsylvanians release about 19 pounds of carbon dioxide into the air for every gallon of gas they use driving. The problem has grown worse in recent years by the rising popularity of sport utility vehicles, which belch almost twice as much carbon dioxide as a mid-sized car.

Pennsylvanians use twice as much energy, per person, as the English or the French, and three times as much as the Poles or the Spanish.

But these differences pale in comparison to the huge gulf in energy consumption between Pennsylvania and Third World countries. Pennsylvanians use about 16 times as much energy, per person, as the Indians or the Pakistanis. While Pennsylvania averages about two motor vehicles for every household, China has one car for every thousand households.

As the global economy evolves, affluent countries cannot maintain extravagantly consumptive lifestyles while expecting developing countries to restrain their appetites and conserve their resources. If Third World people begin consuming resources at anywhere near the rate of Pennsylvanians, the impact on the global environment will be swift, calamitous, and irreversible. Yet developing countries are diligently trying to follow our example.

Car ownership in China has more than doubled since 1997, and car production in China has grown to two million units per year. With its economy growing at an average rate of 8 percent a year, the Chinese car market is expected to jump 30 percent a year.

In 1991, the National Academy of Sciences said the United States should act promptly to reduce the threat

ENERGY CONSUMPTION PER CAPITA,
SELECTED COUNTRIES
(Measured in Metric Tons Oil Equivalent)

UNITED STATES	
SWEDEN	
GERMANY	
JAPAN	
BRITAIN	
POLAND	
MEXICO	
CHINA	
INDIA	
ETHIOPIA	

0   1000   2000   3000   4000   5000   6000   7000   8000

Source: World Resources Institute

34

of global warming by reducing the burning of fossil fuels. Not only have we failed to do so, U.S. emissions have actually grown by 13 percent since then. More than 1,600 scientists, including 102 Nobel laureates, have signed a World Scientists' Warning to Humanity stating that "A new ethic is required, a new attitude toward discharging our responsibility for caring for ourselves and for the earth" if environmental catastrophe is to be avoided. That will require changing the lifestyle of every Pennsylvanian.

As Columbia University historian Kenneth T. Jackson says, "The United States is not only the world's first suburban nation, but it will also be its last. The earth cannot sustain any more economies like ours."

Photo © Tom Kelly

Above: A Philadelphia policeman employs an energy-efficient method to patrol Germantown Avenue.

Left: A news carrier uses pedal power to deliver the Pottstown Mercury to his customers.

Photo © Tom Kelly

But many Pennsylvanians find themselves lapsing into ever more wasteful lifestyles.

Killing the goose that lays the golden eggs?

Lancaster County is the richest non-irrigated farming county in America. It out produces ten states, including every state in New England.

Remarkably, Lancaster County has none of the giant agribusinesses that dominate the Midwest and the West. The county's 4,500 farms are small, family-owned enterprises, many operated by the Plain Sects. The bounty comes not from technology, but from reverence for the land. Lancaster County farmers are deeply committed to a 250-year tradition of stewardship that has increased the fertility of the soil and the beauty of the terrain. The landscapes are rich, peaceful, seemingly eternal.

And they are being destroyed.

Tourist businesses have spread randomly all over the county, destroying or driving away the very things the tourists have come to see. Factory outlets have proliferated from a handful of backlot buildings to more than 200 full-blown stores scattered about the countryside, each beckoning customers with big signs and bigger parking lots. Scores of companies, large and small, have relocated to the "country," bringing thousands of employees and dozens of housing projects in their wake. Formerly bucolic vistas are now pocked with boxy housing subdivisions. Industrial parks straddle pastureland, bringing tractor-trailers to the same narrow roads as horse-drawn buggies. Route 30, for centuries the main east-west artery through the county, is walled in with tourist meccas, from the Dutch Wonderland Family Fun Park to the car-packed Rockvale Square Outlet Center, the highest volume outlet of its kind in America.

Since 1960, Lancaster County has lost more than 90,000 acres of farmland, an area more than twice the size of Pittsburgh, to sprawling development. Scores of Plain Sect families who can no longer farm in the county have moved to New York, Kentucky, and other less developed regions.

Much of Lancaster County's explosive growth has come at the expense of the city of Lancaster. Once the county's cultural, retail, commercial, and residential hub, Lancaster is now in serious decline. The city has lost thousands of residents, thousands of jobs, and is increasingly a refuge for minorities and the poor. The city's population has gone from 95 percent white in 1960 to 55 percent non-Hispanic white and 45 percent black and Hispanic today. More than half the children in the Lancaster City School District come from low-income families.

For most of its history, Lancaster County has truly been a paradise on earth. Now it is self-destructing.

Left: A huge outlet center elbows its way into prime Lancaster County farmland.

Below: Houses surround a Lancaster County farm.

An Amish farmer contends with traffic congestion.

The decline of our cities was not inevitable

Many people believe the growth of the suburban nation, with the consequent decline of our cities and towns, is simply the free market in action. Not true. Until the state and federal governments adopted a series of misguided policies that encouraged them to leave, Pennsylvanians enjoyed city and town life.

Here are some examples.

For decades after World War II, the Federal Housing Administration and the Veterans Administration zealously promoted suburbia at the expense of cities. In insuring the home mortgages for millions of Americans, the FHA and VA gave preferential ratings to suburban homes over city homes by favoring new construction, and by setting standards, such as side yard and setback requirements, that were impossible to meet in the cities.

When large numbers of blacks migrated from the South to take jobs in Pennsylvania cities, the government responded with policies to "redline" — refuse to insure mortgages — in neighborhoods where blacks lived. Unscrupulous real estate agents engaged in racial "block-busting" tactics designed to frighten residents into selling their homes "while you still can." Huge sections of Philadelphia "tipped" from overwhelmingly white to overwhelmingly black in just a few years. Judges further encouraged white flight by ordering the desegregation of city schools while excluding suburban schools.

The government promoted the construction of low-income public housing projects in Pennsylvania cities, but allowed suburban municipalities to avoid them. This accelerated the concentration of poor people in the cities.

"Urban renewal" clearance programs demolished long-established neighborhoods in cities like Erie, Reading, and Altoona for projects that failed or never materialized.

The federal and state governments poured millions of taxpayer dollars into new highways that encouraged the outward movement of residents and industries from the cities, yet declined to put funds into the public transportation that cities depend on.

Environmental regulations made it prohibitively expensive to redevelop older industrial areas, encouraging businesses to develop pristine rural areas for new housing, offices, and industrial parks.

Collection of Bucks County Historical Society

Although the Pennsylvania General Assembly passed legislation in 1995 to encourage the reuse of "brownfield" sites, it is still less expensive and less troublesome for industry to develop virgin fields. State agencies like PennVEST have fostered this process by financing the construction of new water and sewer systems in semi-rural areas of Pennsylvania.

Even building codes have worked against established towns by making it prohibitively expensive to renovate older buildings.

Pennsylvania's heavy reliance on the local real estate tax encourages suburban and semi-rural municipalities to promote widespread development to gain higher tax revenues. At the same time, cities are forced to raise their taxes to pay for increased police and social service costs, which provokes residents to leave for the suburbs, where taxes are lower.

When all these hidden subsidies for suburban living are considered, together with the penalties for city and town dwelling, the mystery is not that Pennsylvania's cities and towns have declined. The mystery is that they have survived at all.

Left: Short-sighted government policies encouraged middle class people to leave the cities after World War II for new suburbs like Levittown in Bucks County.

Below: At the same time, the concentration of poor people into public housing projects like these high-rises in North Philadelphia, now abandoned, degraded city neighborhoods throughout Pennsylvania.

The new economic reality

But a new day is dawning, and today, Pennsylvanians face a new financial reality. The days of lavish spending are over. Like the rest of America, Pennsylvania was sitting on top of the world in 1945. Global warfare had left other industrialized nations in a shambles, but the United States was stronger than ever, producing three-quarters of all the goods on earth. For the next three decades — until the early 1970s — Americans enjoyed unprecedented gains in living standards. The average family's real income nearly doubled. The blue collar worker at Bethlehem Steel or white collar manager at Westinghouse came to expect lifetime job security and a good pension.

No more. Low-skilled manufacturing jobs have moved to Asia and Latin American or been eliminated by automation. Many skilled jobs are starting to migrate to low-wage nations like India, which has a huge pool of English speaking natives and more than two million college graduates per year. Even IBM, for example, expects to shift white collar jobs overseas to keep costs down. Within America, businesses are relying more on part-time employees who receive low wages and few benefits.

It's inevitable that American incomes will languish while other nations catch up, says Donald Fites, former chairman of Caterpillar, which closed its huge York County plant in 1998. "I don't think it is realistic for Americans to control so much of the world's gross national product," he explains.

Although family income rose in the 1990s, especially for the well-educated, the overall gains for most working and middle class families have been modest since the early 1970s. In fact, many economists say, family incomes have risen mostly because

people are working longer hours, and because more wives and mothers are in the workplace. Where one wage-earner used to support most middle class families in the 1950s, it now takes two. And half of all Americans have nothing saved toward retirement.

Private industry and government have increasingly mortgaged the future to pay today's bills. Company pension plans covering 44 million Americans are underfunded by more than $300 billion, and most state pension plans are underfunded as well.

Since 1980, the federal government has gone on a colossal borrowing binge, quintupling the federal debt to $6 trillion, with a projected debt of $8.6 trillion by 2008.

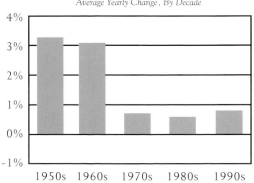

AMERICAN MEDIAN FAMILY INCOME
Average Yearly Change, By Decade

Ending nearly seventy years as the mainstay of the city, Bethlehem Steel closed its Johnstown plant in late 1992. For most of the twentieth century, Bethlehem Steel was the nation's second-largest steel producer, but fierce competition from abroad drove the company into bankruptcy in 2001. When Bethlehem Steel sold its assets to International Steel Co. in 2003, its workforce had shrunk from 165,000 employees in the late 1950s to 11,000. The company cut off health and pension benefits to its 95,000 retirees when it sold out to International Steel. Thirty-eight U.S. steel companies have filed for bankruptcy protection since 1997.

Meanwhile, the government's major entitlement program, Social Security, faces enormous financial problems. Unless taxes are raised substantially or benefits reduced dramatically, Social Security will run short of funds about 2030, when there will be just two workers for every retiree.

All of these problems we refuse to acknowledge. Rather than adopt a more modest lifestyle, we have spent to the max and placed the tab on our children's credit cards.

The true costs of sprawl

In the same fashion, we refuse to acknowledge the true costs of our sprawling style of development. It is extremely expensive to build and maintain. With each passing decade since the 1950s, Pennsylvania developers have consumed increasing quantities of land for each new home or office built. Between 1982 and 1997, when the state's population grew just 2.5 percent, the amount of developed land increased an astonishing 47 percent.

Each new mile of highway, electric and telephone line, and water and sewer pipe serves fewer people than ever before. It's all subsidized by the ratepayer and the taxpayer at enormous expense.

Florida, one of the fastest growing states in America, appointed a task force in 1988 to study which land-use patterns were most cost effective. Dr. James Frank, professor of urban and regional planning at Florida State University, reviewed every major postwar study of development costs in the United States and Great Britain. Frank, whose findings were published by the Urban Land Institute, found that traditional towns cost only a third to a half as much for roads, sewers, and other infrastructure as suburban sprawl. They are also much less expensive for government services ranging from police and fire protection to mail delivery.

People who live in low-density suburbs, especially those far from the perimeter of existing development, receive huge indirect subsidies from the rest of the public, Frank says. If suburbanites were to pay the full costs of their lifestyles, they would be paying more for roads, because they drive longer distances; and more for electric, telephone and sewer service, because of the longer transmission distances and higher lot frontage costs.

It's commonly assumed Americans are so enamored of the suburban lifestyle that they would never accept any other living pattern. But, Frank says, no one knows how many people would switch if they had to bear the full costs of that lifestyle.

For example, American motorists and truckers receive billions of dollars in subsidies every year. "Gasoline taxes and user charges cover less than two-thirds of all the tangible costs" of highways, writes Columbia University professor Sigurd Grava, and even less if the costs of parking, pollution, and vehi-

cle accidents are included. In Europe, where a much higher percentage of people walk or use mass transit than in Pennsylvania, driving is not similarly subsidized by government.

A year after it began its study, Florida's task force recommended that the state reign in suburbia and promote more traditional, town-like development. Florida amended its state plan in 1993, encouraging local governments to promote compact development and discourage sprawl.

Many people may find this an attractive scene, but sprawling development like this in Chester County is destroying our farmland and open space. Such land-use patterns increased the amount of developed land in Pennsylvania by 47 percent between 1982 and 1997, while the population increased just 2.5 percent. Experts say sprawl is far more costly to build and maintain than traditional towns.

The future is ours to determine

Pennsylvania, too, needs to reassess the costs of sprawl. Are we willing to accept the continued degradation of our environment and the further deterioration of our cities?

Are we resigned to a world of increasing fear and alienation, of haves and have-nots, of dwindling public resources and increasing social problems?

Do we want the continued stress of having to pay for oversized homes in remote subdivisions, straining our budgets and forcing us to spend ever more time driving from place to place?

It doesn't have to be this way. By rearranging our homes and workplaces, we can avert the loss of any more scenic landscapes and open space. We can substantially reduce our cost of living. We can create communities that are close-knit and attractive — where children walk to school and play safely in the local park.

The hardest part is believing it can be done. "We have a hard time thinking about what we want, what the future should be," says Robert Bendick, who led a successful movement to save open space as environmental commissioner in Rhode Island. "We seem to be better at talking about what we don't like." As a result, Bendick says, "We often seem to settle for things that don't come out very well because they're a compilation of what people don't want."

Let's not be trapped by the negative thinking of the past. Pennsylvania is loaded with bright, resourceful people. We just need to get organized.

Planning
for the Future

Shortly after World War II, Dutch scholar Fred Polak wrote a book called *The Image of the Future*. Examining the major movements of western civilization, such as Christianity and the golden age of Greece, Polak concluded that great cultures evolved because their people shared a powerful and positive image of their future.

In recent years, a small but growing number of states have begun thinking positively about their future. It remains to be seen whether their cultures will be great, but in each, the people have attempted to define the kind of future they want for themselves and initiated a comprehensive planning effort to bring it about.

In many states, this movement has become known as "smart growth."

Initially, these states had differing motivations for developing plans. Georgians, for example, wanted to encourage economic development. New Jerseyans felt choked by traffic congestion. Vermonters wanted to protect and preserve their postcard-perfect villages and towns. Marylanders wanted to stop the pollution of the Chesapeake Bay.

Once these states began the process of planning, however, they realized it offered other benefits. For the first time, citizens were encouraged to think about the kind of future they wanted for themselves and their children. For the first time, the government was trying to coordinate the actions of all state agencies, local municipalities, and school districts toward a common, articulated goal.

States that have adopted comprehensive plans usually began the planning process with blue-ribbon panels appointed by the governor or the legislature. In Vermont, for example, the governor appointed a twelve-member Commission on Vermont's Future. The commission held public hearings across the state and met with more than 2,000 residents, ranging from chamber of commerce directors to housewives. These state panels attempted to define a vision for the future. And from Maryland to Washington state, they reached remarkably similar conclusions. The people want:

- Economic development to provide a steady source of jobs.
- Revival of their cities and towns, making them safe and attractive places to live.
- Protection of farmland and open spaces.
- Housing everyone can afford, right down to a person earning the minimum wage.
- Good government services at the least cost.
- A sense of community.

These ideals may seem obvious. But only a handful of states have defined them as goals and established strategies to achieve them. And most of these states, after considerable research and public discussion, have reached remarkably similar conclusions about what they need. They need to build communities, not sprawl.

Mural, Pennsylvania House of Representatives

Cities, villages, and towns: A sensible way of life

For 6,000 years of recorded history, people have lived in cities, villages, and towns, and for good reason: They were efficient, economical, sociable, and often beautiful. According to Columbia University historian Kenneth T. Jackson, cities and towns shared five characteristics:

They were compact: In 1819, the year Queen Victoria was born, London was the largest city in the world with 800,000 residents. Yet people on the city's fringes, like Kensington or Paddington, were only five miles from the center of the city. That's little more than an hour's walk.

There was a clear distinction between city and country: At the end of a city or town was a clear boundary where the countryside began. There were no houses or restaurants stretched endlessly along the highways between villages, and no isolated developments scattered among farms and forests.

There was a mixture of functions: Houses, stores, public buildings, workplaces, taverns, schools and parks were interspersed. There were no zones given over exclusively to one function.

Most people lived within walking distance of work: In even the largest cities, most people lived less than a mile — a fifteen-minute walk — from where they worked. Many artisans and professionals such as doctors and lawyers lived in the same house where they worked.

The best homes were closest to the center: The most fashionable people of any city or town lived closest to the center, where the palaces and churches and best stores were located. This is still true in Europe, South America, and many other areas of the world.

Historians Will and Ariel Durant spent their lifetimes researching and writing their eleven-volume *Story of Civilization.* Then, in their late 70s, they concluded their work with a short addendum called *Lessons of History.* One lesson, they said, is that for every hundred new ideas, "ninety-nine or more will probably be inferior to the traditional responses which they propose to replace."

In the whole sweep of civilization, America's fifty-year experiment with isolation and sprawl is but a few ticks on the clock. To many Pennsylvanians, suburbia seems a natural way of life. It is, in fact, an aberration. Cities, villages and towns are the rule.

As these early twentieth century postcards show, Pennsylvania towns were compact, pedestrian-friendly, and surrounded by open space.

Downtown Scranton had houses, stores and offices in th

Wilkes-Barre's public square was lined with stores and a

There was a clear demarcation between the city of Bradford and the countryside surrounding it.

Residents of Lancaster could easily walk to their jobs at the Hamilton Watch Co., foreground.

Children walk home from school in Letchworth Garden City.

Above: The downtown shopping district in Letchworth Garden City. In England, two-thirds of all retail business is still conducted in traditional downtowns.

Right: My father took this photo of the Berkshire Knitting Mills, a part of Wyomissing Industries, in 1944. Wyomissing Industries proved that even manufacturing plants could be beautiful and compatible with nearby residential neighborhoods.

Compact and beautiful

Nevertheless, many Pennsylvanians have a fear of moderate- to high-density housing located near stores and workplaces. It's an unjustified fear. In virtually every other country of the world, including our northern neighbor, Canada, people routinely live in such communities.

I am not talking about Third World densities. Nor am I talking about the densities of American and European cities at the turn of the century, when families were packed together in tenement housing at rate of 250,000 people per square mile.

But it is possible to house people close enough together — say ten or more dwelling units per acre — to provide a pleasant mix of single family homes, townhouses, and apartments that makes walking and mass transportation feasible. Such a mix can include big homes on large lots, as long as they are counterbalanced with apartment buildings on other lots. This can be accomplished with plenty of private yards and few or no buildings taller than three stories.

Photo by the author

Every neighborhood we build — regardless of housing density — can be beautiful, if we make it so. People in western countries "have been carrying around with them as part of their mental baggage a deeply felt and despairing assumption that progress demands degraded surroundings," writes Tony Hiss in his book, *Experience of Place*. "You put up with such surroundings as long as you have to, and you run away from them as soon as you can afford to; but, this belief has it, deteriorated landscapes and debased communities and bad smells and hideous noises are simply a given — something we all have to live with."

That's simply not true.

There's no reason why our industrial buildings, our commercial and retail buildings, our homes, and our highways can't be beautiful. An example from my own experience is the place my father worked, Wyomissing Industries. In this complex of large brick factories were manufactured women's hosiery, narrow fabrics, and heavy textile machinery. It was a beautiful complex. Ivy covered the walls of the handsome, well-constructed buildings. The streets were paved with brick and lined with Japanese flowering cherry trees. The factories were in fact pleasant neighbors to nearby homes.

Wyomissing Industrics was the hub of the town of Wyomissing, which was laid out in 1912 as one of America's first garden cities.

The term "garden city" was coined a century ago by English visionary Ebenezer Howard, who believed cities could be green and beautiful. According to Howard, the ideal town would have 32,000 residents living on two square miles of land, amid trees and greenery, and surrounded by a four-square-mile "greenbelt" of protected open space. In a garden city, people could live within walking distance of stores and workplaces, but also be able to walk into the countryside. At the center of each garden city would be a train station connecting it to other towns. Unlike most visionaries, Howard actually built two prototypes of his dream — Letchworth Garden City and Welwyn Garden City, two of the loveliest towns in England.

Several garden cities were built in America as well.

Transit-oriented development

All around the country, small communities are being designed around rail stations, following the example of garden cities like Forest Hills Gardens, N.Y., and "streetcar suburbs" like Englewood, N.J.; Narberth, Pa.; and Riverside, Ill. Typically, these commuter towns featured shops, offices, and apartment buildings forming a miniature downtown around a train station. Surrounding this hub were several blocks of homes that gradually increased in size as the distance increased from the center of town.

Planners and developers are reviving this concept along new and old rail lines in a score of metropolitan areas, from San Jose, Calif., to New York City. (The potential for such communities exists in Pennsylvania. Several train and rapid transit lines serve Philadelphia suburbs, and a light rail line connecting Pittsburgh to its suburbs was constructed in the 1980s.)

These "transit villages" extend for a radius of a third to a half-mile from the central transit station to the edge of the community. That's less than a ten-minute walk for most adults. Within this radius, it is possible to place a small commercial district with stores, day care, and offices centered around a transit station and a small park. This core area is surrounded by several blocks of small apartment buildings, townhouses, and individual homes. Transit villages can be anywhere from fifty to three hundred acres, the size of Main Line villages like Bryn Mawr or

Paoli. They can house anywhere from hundreds to thousands of residents. Several of them can be developed along one rail line, like a loose string of pearls, encouraging residents to travel between villages.

Studies of existing areas similar to transit villages indicate they will dramatically reduce auto traffic. One study, for example, showed that residents of Rockridge, a 1920s streetcar suburb of Oakland, Calif., drove half as many miles annually as residents of Danville, a modern suburb 15 miles west of Oakland.

In recent years, millions of dollars have been invested to build transit villages in metropolitan Portland, the San Francisco Bay area, the Baltimore-Washington area, and Atlanta. Perhaps the most suc-cessful transit villages are located along the Washington Metro commuter rail line in Arlington, Virginia, where thousands of homes, offices, and shops have been built in the last decade.

New Jersey has officially designated eight communities, such as Morristown and Metuchen, as transit villages eligible for state funding to revitalize the areas surrounding their train stations and provide amenities like bus shelters and bike racks.

"Today, good development sites around transit are like the highway exits used to be in the 1960s," says Boston developer Tony Pangaro. "Back then, if you knew where the highway exit was going to be, you bought and built. Much the same is happening today with transit systems."

Drawing by Alan MacBain

Right: Separated bike lanes complement nearly every road in the Netherlands.
Below: A family bikes through the village of Hastrecht. (Photos by the author)

Above, left to right: A tot rides with her grandfather; the main street in Driebergen, as in most Dutch towns, provides separate lanes for cars, bicycles and pedestrians; the local supermarket provides parking for bicycles rather than cars. (Photos by the author)

Walking and bicycling

Mass transportation consumes far less energy and space than cars, but for short trips there are even better ways to get around: walking and bicycling.

One quarter of all trips in America cover less than a mile. Most people can walk a mile in fifteen minutes, and on a bicycle, such a trip takes five to eight minutes. Walking and bicycling instead of driving saves people money and reduces the need for expansive (and expensive) highways and parking lots.

Walking and bicycling as part of daily life can also improve our health. More than half of all Americans are overweight — double the percentage of just thirty years ago — and obesity is second only to smoking as the leading cause of premature death. The Centers for Disease Control recommends Americans should exercise at least a half hour daily to prevent diabetes, heart disease, and other illnesses.

In western Europe, says John Pucher, a Rutgers University transportation expert, anywhere from 16 to 46 percent of all trips in metro areas are made by walking or riding a bicycle. That's an enormous amount of energy saved, air pollution prevented, and traffic congestion eliminated.

The Dutch, for example, have implemented a wide range of policies during the last two decades to simultaneously encourage walking and bicycling while dramatically increasing bicycle and pedestrian safety.

"In the 1970s we were building more highways to ease congestion," says Dutch planner Harry van Veneendaal," but as the highways just filled up with cars, we realized they were only a temporary solution and not sustainable. So we stopped the policy of just giving into motorists."

In the Netherlands, dedicated bicycle lanes adjoin virtually every street, and many lead places cars cannot go. Cycling is routine for folks for all ages: children, young people (even on dates!), men in business suits, carefully coiffed women, the elderly.

In fact, nearly half of all trips are made by walking or riding a bicycle. This means Dutch cities and towns are not checkerboarded with surface parking lots. It means they are quiet. It means the streets are alive with people, integrating the old and young to a degree seldom seen in this country.

In Amsterdam, you can safely ride a bicycle from the heart of the downtown to open countryside in twenty-five minutes. Residents of smaller cities and towns are five to ten minutes from green pastures.

"There's no reason we can't build dedicated bicycle lanes and take other measures to integrate walking and bicycling into the daily routines of Americans," Pucher says. "That's the best way to ensure adequate levels of daily exercise."

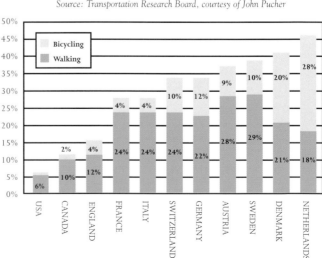

Walking and Bicycling Shares of Urban Travel , 1995
Source: Transportation Research Board, courtesy of John Pucher

Country	Walking	Bicycling
USA	6%	—
CANADA	10%	2%
ENGLAND	12%	4%
FRANCE	24%	4%
ITALY	24%	4%
SWITZERLAND	24%	10%
GERMANY	22%	12%
AUSTRIA	28%	9%
SWEDEN	29%	10%
DENMARK	21%	20%
NETHERLANDS	18%	28%

A world-class corporate center that makes sense...

Pittsburgh boasts one of the most compact and dynamic downtowns of any city in the world: the Golden Triangle. On fewer than 400 acres, not even a square mile, the Golden Triangle comprises a complete city with 140,000 jobs and 2,700 residents.

The Golden Triangle boasts a wonderful old department store and specialty stores, hotels, theaters, restaurants, and the spectacular thirty-five-acre Point State Park, all within fifteen minutes' walking distance of each other.

Because the Golden Triangle is so compact, more than half of its workers either walk or take mass transit — buses or light rail — to their jobs. As a result, the downtown has not been decimated for parking lots. Once at work, people can walk to lunch, to meetings at other businesses, and on errands. They can also take the subway, which is free downtown. The Golden Triangle is a world-class example of a working environment that is walkable, cosmopolitan, and breathtakingly beautiful, close to a wide variety of residential areas, and easily accessible by foot, car, train, plane, or bus. It represents the most safe, efficient, and environmentally friendly way of arranging workplaces on a large scale that humans have ever devised.

Right: Pittsburgh's Golden Triangle is one of the most beautiful and efficient corporate centers in the world. It contains about 140,000 jobs, all within walking distance of each other.

Below: Office workers walk on lunchtime errands at Market Square in the Golden Triangle.

And one that doesn't

In contrast, I give you the Great Valley Corporate Center. Constructed in the 1970s and 1980s north of Route 202 in suburban Chester County, fifteen miles west of Philadelphia, the Great Valley Corporate Center occupies more land — about 650 acres — than Pittsburgh's Golden Triangle, but with far less efficiency.

Because Great Valley is remote from any residential neighborhoods, no one can walk to work. Because each office building is sited, alone, on a huge, manicured plot, mass transportation is difficult to provide. Because of its low density, Great Valley employs fewer than 15,000 workers, a small fraction of the number employed in the Golden Triangle. Because most employees drive to work in separate cars, the parking lots take up more space than the office buildings themselves.

As you might expect, there are no sidewalks at Great Valley. There's hardly any place you can walk to. You cannot walk to lunch or for shopping. You cannot walk on errands or to meetings in other office buildings. Once you're there, you can't go anywhere else without getting back into a car. As a consequence, there is none of the vibrancy, diversity, beauty, or convenience of a downtown. Great Valley is a well-maintained but bland wasteland — lackluster buildings surrounded by hundreds and hundreds and hundreds of cars.

Left: The Great Valley Corporate Center, shown with adjacent corporate buildings, sprawls over 650 acres and employs fewer than 15,000 workers. People are almost totally dependent on the car to get around.

Below: In place of squares and sidewalks, Great Valley has a wide variety of parking lots.

Photo © Tom Kelly

The richness of a city

Do you know what is most distressing about barren corporate parks like Great Valley? It's that they're sucking the resources out of existing cities. Great cities. Philadelphia, just a few miles east of Great Valley, has traditionally been a rich business, civic, cultural, social, educational and residential environment. Many tenants of corporate centers like Great Valley moved from there. Just what did they flee?

Center City Philadelphia, laid out by William Penn in 1682, stretches from South Street to Vine Street, from the Schuylkill River to the Delaware River. It covers only about two square miles of land, which means the longest distance from one point to another is about a forty-minute walk.

Some 80,000 people live within this area, many of them in single family houses or small apartment buildings. There are 300,000 jobs of every description in the area. Center City Philadelphia includes more retail stores, of much richer variety, than any mall in Pennsylvania. It includes thousands of offices, large and small; unobtrusive manufacturing plants; beautiful residential sections such as Society Hill, Old City, and Rittenhouse Square; hotels and bed and breakfasts; numerous green spaces, including Independence National Historical Park and Penn's Landing; major libraries, museums, and colleges; restaurants and theaters; hospitals and medical schools, and public institutions ranging from elementary schools to the federal courthouse.

Cars are not needed to get around. If the walk is too far, there are buses, trolleys, and subways. The scenery includes some of the finest vistas in America.

Center City Philadelphia is cleaner and safer than most American downtowns. But if it had the resources of European or Canadian cities, it would surely be one of the safest and most attractive places in the world.

If it were like Paris, for example, the streets would be swept by hand. Every day. Trash would be collected seven days a week. Mail would be delivered three times a day. Subway trains would arrive at your station every 80 seconds during rush hour. Such is the character of municipal services in Paris.

The French national government pays 40 percent of the city's budget, covers almost all welfare costs, and pays the salaries of Paris's teachers, policemen, and firefighters. The city works because the French make it work. Can Pennsylvanians say the same for the birthplace of modern democracy?

Above: Thousands of residents are within easy walking distance of The Gallery, Philadelphia's four-story indoor shopping center. A commuter rail stop is on the lowest level.

Right: Philadelphians of all ages enjoy a beautiful fall day under the trees of Rittenhouse Square.

Clockwise from above: The shopping district of West Chester; downtown State College; Victorian homes in Bellefonte; the shops of Lewisburg; a shady residential neighborhood in Mt. Lebanon.

Pennsylvania's traditional towns

Some of the loveliest towns in Pennsylvania —
Philadelphia's Chestnut Hill; Main Line communities
like Ardmore and Bryn Mawr; courthouse towns like
Doylestown and Meadville; college towns like
Lewisburg and State College; and Pittsburgh streetcar
suburbs like Dormont and Mount Lebanon — have
mixtures of homes, stores, and offices that are dense
enough to support walking and public transportation.

If new communities were built at the same densities as these towns, Pennsylvania could curb the
auto, stop the loss of farmland and open space, and
provide decent housing for residents of all incomes.

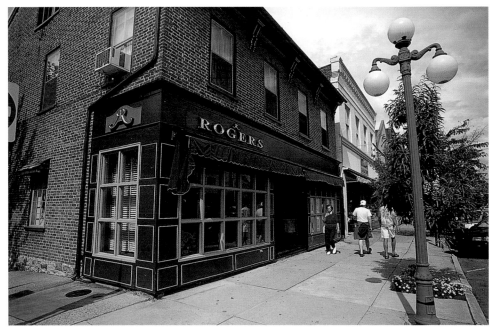

The old-fashioned American dream

By now you are asking yourself: Is this guy talking to an empty room, or do people really want these kinds of cities and towns? Aren't people voting with their pocketbooks when they buy in suburbia?

A man with a well-researched idea of what Americans want is Tony Nelessen, a Princeton, N.J., architect and Rutgers University professor. "What I was taught at Harvard thirty years ago was that you as the planner superimposed your ideas on the community," Nelessen says. "I've since learned that's not the way to do it. You let the residents design their own community."

In the last several years, he's been enlisted by communities from Arkansas to Oregon to write zoning codes encouraging traditional neighborhoods. On each assignment, Nelessen begins by showing residents 240 slides of various kinds of development. He asks them to rate the slides on a scale from plus 10 to minus 10, based on what they like or don't like.

Americans are yearning for old-fashioned villages and towns, not more suburbia, he says. What people like are charming towns like Princeton and Alexandria, Va. What they hate is what they have: tract housing, strip malls, and corporate centers.

"People want environments that are humane, more pedestrian friendly, more interactive with people," he says. "Because the separation of land uses has been the normal planning dogma for fifty years, people think it's a fantasy to say you can walk to work. We're showing them it's not."

Nelessen has written a traditional zoning ordinance for Lancaster County's Manheim Township, a growing suburban municipality. He based the ordinance on a nearby community that Manheim residents said they love: the 19th century borough of Lititz. The home of Linden Hall, a private school for girls, Sturgis Pretzels, and the Wilbur Chocolate Factory, Lititz has narrow streets, closely spaced homes, and a little downtown graced with a shady park.

Architect Tony Nelessen finds most people favor traditional towns like Princeton, where his office is located.

People rate their preferences

A shopping mall is rated at -2.4.

A traditional town scene earns a +5.39 rating.

These images taken by architect Tony Nelessen are among hundreds that have been evaluated on a scale of -10 to +10 by residents across the country in Nelessen's Visual Preference Surveys.

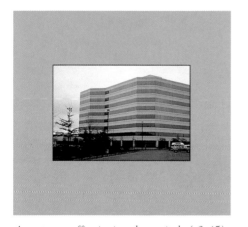

A corporate office is viewed negatively (-2.45).

A pedestrian courtyard looks appealing (+3.5).

Strip development is not popular (-4.56).

But a downtown mall wins kudos (+3.4).

Real villages instead of sprawl

Cranberry Township is a fast-growing municipality in Butler County just north of Pittsburgh. It has a Wal-Mart/Kmart/strip-mall commercial corridor instead of a downtown. It has numerous isolated housing subdivisions spread over twenty-three square miles of land. If you live there, you have to drive everywhere for everything. It is home to about 24,000 people.

There are municipalities like Cranberry Township all over Pennsylvania.

Let's suppose we were to rearrange Cranberry's population into just two villages. We move 6,000 people into one village of 1.4 square miles called Swarthmore. We move 14,000 people into another village of 1.8 square miles called Princeton. Now 85 percent of the residents of Cranberry are living in two villages taking up just 15 percent of its land area, so the rest of Cranberry is truly rural. Not only is this ecologically sound, it is economically sound, because all of Cranberry's infrastructure is concentrated in two compact areas.

In these two villages, the residents are close enough so they can walk to many of the places they need to go. Because 6,000 people are enough to support a public school system, and because these people are living in a small area, the children in each village can walk to school.

There's even room in each village for higher education: Swarthmore College and Princeton University. And because we have a sizable group of people living close together, the villages can support a passenger rail line that goes to the nearest city, and points beyond.

Of course, we're talking about real places. The combined population of Princeton, N.J., and Swarthmore, Pa., is nearly as great as Cranberry Township, but their combined land area, even including the college campuses, is only 15 percent of that of Cranberry Township. Which would we prefer for our state? Princetons and Swarthmores? Or Cranberry Townships?

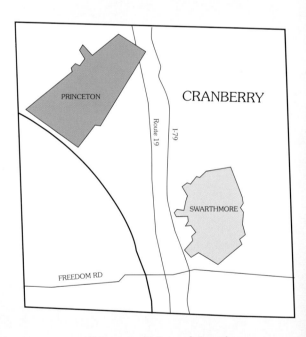

Princeton, N.J., and Swarthmore, Pa., have the same combined population as 85 percent of Cranberry Township's, but they take up only 15 percent as much land.

Left: Most of Swarthmore looks like this shady street. Its homes are within walking distance of a school, stores, and a train station.

Below: Houses sprawl over Cranberry Township hillsides, far from stores and workplaces. Virtually all trips must be made by car.

The return of the small town

Happily, developers are learning important lessons from wonderful villages like Princeton and Swarthmore.

"Society's search for neighborhoods that feature more neighborliness and the type of planning that reduces suburban sprawl are gaining favor with today's new home-buyer," John Schleimer told the *Sacramento Bee*. Schleimer is a real estate analyst in California. He surveyed 619 residents of three recently constructed "neo-traditional" communities. An overwhelming 84 percent of the respondents said that if they had to do it over, they'd again choose a traditional neighborhood rather than a conventional development.

One of these "neo-traditional" communities is The Kentlands, a new town recently built on 350 acres in Gaithersburg, Md. The Kentlands is designed to be a place where people can walk and mingle. It has a town center with an elementary school, a church, and a day-care center. It has a large mall (including a Kmart) within walking distance of every home.

About 100 children already walk to the elementary school, and more walkers are expected as the community grows. "That's a major reason families are moving here," says acting principal Howard Wohl. "Parents like their kids to be able to walk to school."

The blocks are laid out on a grid system like a traditional town, with sidewalks along narrow, tree-lined streets. Each block of The Kentlands has a variety of homes, from townhouses to large, free-standing five-bedroom homes on modest lots. Many of the rear garages have apartments on the second floor.

"I just love the concept," says Jill Loftus, who bought a townhouse close enough to the elementary school to walk with her kindergartner to school. "We love the architecture, the way they're putting houses together to make a nice little community."

Marsha and Tedd Hopp, who are active in the local citizens' group, say they want their two children, aged ten and six, to be independent as they grow up. "We figured by the time they're teens, The Kentlands will be developed enough so they can walk to friends' houses, the movies, and the shopping center by themselves," Marsha says. They like the higher housing densities, she says, "because lots of people are within walking distance. That's a big attraction."

The Kentlands is among hundreds of new villages and towns planned or under construction all across America. Even Walt Disney is building a town, called Celebration, that will eventually house 20,000 residents. Located just south of Disney World, Celebration is designed to have the look and feel of a pre-1940 southern town. Apartments, townhouses, and single family detached houses are within walking distance of a traditional main street with offices and stores. Children can walk to a K-12 public school.

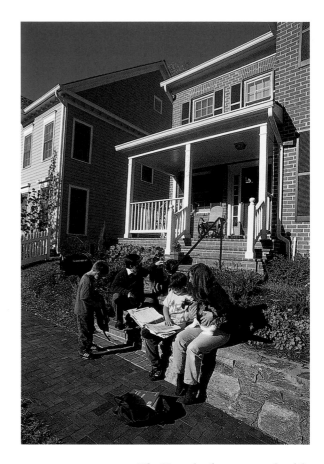

The Hopp family goes over the children's daily schoolwork on the front steps of their home in the Kentlands, Maryland.

Above: Celebration, Florida, has a pedestrian-oriented downtown. Buildings are placed next to the sidewalk, with stores on the first floor and offices or apartments on the upper floors. Parking is behind the buildings.

Left: This neighborhood in Newpoint, a neo-traditional development in Beaufort, South Carolina, looks like it's been around for a century. In fact, these homes were built in the early 1990s.

Photo by the author

Above: The new official map of Cornelius shows where the parks and open space (in green) will be located, and where the interconnecting grid of streets will be constructed as the town is developed. The town center area of Cornelius is shown in red along the proposed light rail line; existing housing is shown in yellow and new residential areas are shown in orange.

Right: Davidson's new land plan code promotes traditional neighborhoods like Lake Davidson Park, now under construction.

Rediscovering the official map

Three fast growing communities in North Carolina have taken Tony Nelessen's ideas one step further. The adjoining towns of Davidson, Cornelius and Huntersville, immediately north of Charlotte, expect their population to increase from 44,000 today to 125,000 in less than twenty years. Rather than see their combined 100 square miles turned into cookie cutter housing tracts and strip malls, the residents of all three municipalities formed committees to control their own destiny.

"Our citizens' committees studied various kinds of development," says Ann Hammond, who directed the development of Huntersville's town plan. "Virtually everyone picked the traditional downtown over the strip shopping center. They wanted neighborhoods with a connected street system rather than isolated cul-de-sac subdivisions."

The towns hired David Walters, professor of urban design at the University of North Carolina, Charlotte, to help them shape their growth. "We went back to the wisdom of the past," Walters says, "which emphasized streets and public spaces as places of shared use. Traditional towns tie homes, stores and workplaces together on a neighborhood scale." To accomplish that goal, all three towns adopted official land development maps.

Official maps are as old as the thirteen colonies. William Penn published one for his "greene Country Towne" of Philadelphia in 1683. Penn designed a rectangular gridiron of 174 blocks and five large parks covering 1,200 acres between the Delaware and Schuylkill Rivers. These 174 blocks were gradually subdivided into smaller building lots for homes, stores, offices as the city grew over the next two centuries.

Until the 1940s, every town in America evolved the same way. A town surveyor would draw up an official map showing where streets would be constructed and building lots created. The map extended beyond the edge of town to cover adjacent farms and open space. When outlying property owners sold their land for development, it would be shaped by the official map.

Sadly, although official maps remain legal in Pennsylvania and elsewhere, this fine system was abandoned after World War II. Developers began

building projects as separate "pods" that were connected only to the nearest highway. No longer were buildings woven into the fabric of a community according to a single coherent plan. They were spread around as aimlessly as litter on a windy day.

The citizen committees in Davidson, Cornelius, and Huntersville began shaping their towns' future appearance by identifying flood plains, steep slopes, and other areas that cannot be developed. They added lands of exceptional beauty they wanted to preserve. These areas were connected on the maps by green corridors consisting of proposed walking and biking trails, parks, schoolyards, and golf courses. Neighborhoods were then defined, together with slightly larger village and town centers. A basic network of streets needed to tie everything together was drawn.

"Enough things fell into place so people could share a vision of what their communities would look like at build-out," Walters says. "Each tract of land became like a piece of a huge jigsaw puzzle, and the official land development map became the equivalent of the picture on the outside of the puzzle box.

Developers can see in advance how their projects will contribute to the overall picture. Residents are assured their towns will evolve efficiently and logically into livable communities."

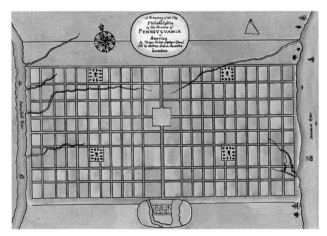

William Penn's 1683 plan for Philadelphia has been followed for 300 years.

Affordable housing in all communities

Another signal distinction of traditional towns like Davidson and new towns like The Kentlands is that they have housing designed for people in every price range (including affordable housing like those apartments above the garages).

To residents of Montgomery County, Maryland, where The Kentlands is located, the idea of building housing for every pocketbook isn't all that distinctive. Since 1974, Montgomery County has required every development of more than fifty units to set aside 12.5 to 15 percent of those homes for low- and moderate-income residents. (Recently, the county lowered the threshold to developments of thirty-five or more units.) This has led to developments like Avenel, which has modest homes for the working poor amid million-dollar mansions. The program is considered the most progressive in the nation. It has enabled people of diverse races and incomes to buy or rent homes in middle and upper class neighborhoods throughout the county. During the last twenty years, Montgomery County's minority population has doubled, to 15 percent black, 11 percent Hispanic, and 11 percent Asian.

The county — it's one of America's wealthiest, by the way — instituted the program because it needed affordable housing, but it didn't want low-income housing concentrated in one area. So far, the policy has created more than 11,000 new affordable housing units. To pay for the subsidized units, developers are given a density bonus, allowing them to build 22 percent more houses than conventional zoning permits. Sixty percent of the homes are earmarked for moderate income families; the rest are divided between the Montgomery County Housing Authority and non-profit housing groups. Because 70 percent of the low-income residents on the county's waiting list are minorities, the program has had the effect of promoting racial integration as well as economic integration. "Our affordable housing is dispersed all over the county," says one official.

The initial decision to require affordable housing in every major development was "agonizing," says William Sher, a former member of Montgomery County Council, the county's governing body. It turned out to be one of the best moves the county ever made. "We've had virtually no negative impact socially," he says.

In fact, a study by one of the county's leading builders, William L. Berry & Co., showed that houses in developments with county-mandated affordable housing appreciated at the same rate or faster than houses in developments without them.

One reason, the developer speculated, might be that developments with more than fifty dwelling units, in addition to having mandated affordable housing, also tend to have amenities such as swimming pools and tennis courts. But clearly, the study said, "the existence of moderately priced dwelling units in a community does not slow home appreciation rates as compared to communities without them."

In Pennsylvania — as elsewhere in America — one of the major obstructions to productive, positive change is our ideas and attitudes about "property rights." To make these new-old towns and cities possible, we've got to come to grips with the disparity between the popular concept of property rights and the reality of property rights.

70

Above: Affordable housing, foreground, is placed within view of million-dollar mansions at the Avenel development in Montgomery County, Md.

Left: The Normandy Crest development has subsidized townhouses, right, across the street from market rate townhouses, left, and close to homes valued at more than $500,000, center.

Property rights and responsibilities

As the world population grows and stronger measures are needed to protect the environment, our ideas about "property rights" must change. As Theodore Roosevelt wrote, "Every man holds his property subject to the general right of the community to regulate its use to whatever degree the public welfare might require."

Unlike Roosevelt, many property owners insist on viewing land as a profit-making commodity that they have an inalienable right to "develop." Farmland and open space are considered temporary uses until something better comes along. Short-sighted government policies in Pennsylvania and other states have encouraged this illusion by zoning millions of acres of land — land that should never be developed — for houses, offices, or industry. As a result, development is happening at random, not where it should.

In fact, no one has ever had a constitutional right

"to do whatever I want with my land." Since the 1920s, both state and federal courts have held that states may zone land in the best interests of the community, as long as zoning does not remove all of the land's economic value. Despite the claims of some "property rights" zealots, the most recent decisions of the U.S. Supreme Court have never wavered from that legal doctrine.

In European nations such as Sweden, France, and Germany, land has traditionally been regarded as a limited commodity that should only be developed in the public interest. England's 1947 Town and Country Planning Act, and subsequent amendments, requires most land to remain as it is. The citizens — not individual property owners — keep for themselves the right to decide when and where land can be built upon. Only designated land around existing settlements may be developed, leaving much of the countryside looking as it did a century ago. The English have planned on a national and countywide basis to require a settlement pattern of cities, villages, and towns surrounded by open countryside.

All private property rights are completely dependent on the community. We maintain a right to our land only because we can record a deed at the county courthouse, which is supported by the community. We enforce our property rights through a legal system supported by the community. Our property would be worthless without roads and electric and telephone lines built by the community. We are safe and secure in our homes because of police and fire departments organized by the community.

Just as the community makes it possible for us to enjoy our property, each community has the right — the obligation, in fact — to ensure private property is used in ways that will benefit the long-term public interest.

Bath, England. Thanks to far-sighted land-use laws, countries like England, France and Germany have maintained the integrity of their towns, farmland, and open space.

Photo © Ernest Frankl

The spirit of community

The term community has come up again and again in this book. I've pointed out that again and again, people articulate a desire for "a sense of community." A community is not just the proper physical arrangement of buildings and roads, although that has been the essential ingredient missing for years in Pennsylvania. A community is also a state of mind.

The rise of amorphous suburbs and the decline of real places to call home has caused many Pennsylvanians to lose their feelings of community. Many residents believe that home ends with the front lawn, and paying taxes is all the community has a right to ask. Many assume that financial success brings with it a right to escape from the poor and all their troubles. But in an enlightened democracy, everyone has an equal responsibility to share common problems and help solve them.

In World War II, no American avoided making a contribution because of status or wealth. Everyone shared the burden. Memorials in our schools and town squares testify to the tremendous sacrifices earlier generations made for something bigger than themselves: the common good.

Studies of World War II combat found that soldiers fought primarily on behalf of the six or seven men around them, a finding that has been validated time and again by subsequent research. It is human nature to care far more about those who live around us than society in the abstract. The military draft benefited America by bringing together people of many races and classes who otherwise would never have met, but formed lifelong friendships when they did.

Preaching on a crowded ship off the coast of Massachusetts in 1630, Governor John Winthrop described the "City upon a Hill" that his fellow Puritans hoped to fashion in the New World: "We must delight in each other, make each other's conditions our own, rejoice together, mourn together, labor and suffer together, always having before our eyes our Community as members of the same body, so we will keep the unity of spirit in the bond of peace." That same spirit of caring and mutual responsibility was the heart and soul of William Penn's "Holy Experiment" for Pennsylvania.

We live in a Commonwealth. Every Pennsylvania law, every state policy, should be considered in the light of encouraging community and mutual responsibility, not diminishing it. No Pennsylvania developer, for example, should ever be permitted to build a housing development for just one income group. We all have an obligation to live in communities that reflect the diversity of our state, and if they are not safe and attractive,

to help make them so. We need to emphasize the importance of public courtesy and consideration for others in our neighborhoods. The only reason we enjoy our free civilization is because of the hard effort of thousands of men and women who went before us. The only way we can repay them is to leave a better world for those who come after us.

Public school community service

"Schools were created to develop good citizens," says Cathy Brill of Maryland's education department. "The way to learn to be a good citizen is not to read about it but to do it." With that in mind, Maryland requires unpaid community service of all public school students. Between sixth grade and graduation, all students must perform at least seventy-five hours of service such as cleaning up parks or tutoring children.

Pennsylvania's Bethlehem Area School District and Keystone Oaks School District also require students to complete unpaid community service before they can graduate from high school — a minimum of 60 hours in Bethlehem and 120 hours at Keystone Oaks.

"I believe we need to teach students that it is not just their privilege to volunteer if they feel so inclined," explains former Bethlehem school board member Robert Thompson, who helped start the program. "As citizens of a democracy they have the responsibility to contribute something of their talent toward the welfare of the whole, to return to the community part of all that they have been given by the community."

The school district has certified more than 125 agencies for the program, including the YMCA, the city recycling agency, elementary schools, Little Leagues, museums, and nursing homes.

Although many students resent the service at first, they often change their minds after they become involved. "I thought it would be a waste," said one student who served at a day-care center, "but I fell into something I loved. I wound up doing triple the requirement."

Public events like the annual Halloween parade in York are among the few activities that bring together nearly everyone in the community.

Ten Rules for a
Quality Community

We need to build real communities in Pennsylvania, not loose accumulations of buildings, highways, and parking lots. Virtually every problem we have — crime, chronic poverty, the degradation of our cities, the loss of farmland and open space, pollution, traffic congestion, the high cost of living — could be solved or greatly alleviated by building real communities.

Just as our government rests upon a few fundamental rules enunciated in the Constitution, a quality community is based on a few simple principles that should be encouraged in a state plan. These principles are the basis of smart growth:

1. A sense of place

Communities — cities, villages, and towns — should have clearly defined boundaries. They shouldn't overrun the countryside.

Pennsylvania's landscapes belong to all of us. They are profoundly important to our lives. When a wooded hillside is slashed by a high-tension line, when a beautiful farm is supplanted by a housing subdivision, when a strip mall seemingly erupts along a public highway, we all suffer from the visual blight. We are all diminished by the loss of our shared natural heritage.

There is no reason we should tolerate the degradation of our land. Benton MacKaye, an American forester and planner who first envisioned the Appalachian Trail, proposed in the late 1920s that the land within 500 feet of all highway rights-of-way be zoned to permit only agricultural or forestry uses. People should live and work in towns, he said, not scattered along the roadsides. His idea for limited-access highways was eagerly adopted. His complementary proposal for limiting highway development, unfortunately, was not.

We can best protect our landscapes by returning to Pennsylvania's traditional pattern of distinctive villages and towns surrounded by open, unblemished vistas. English cities and towns are nestled inside Green Belts, rings of pristine open land from five to twenty miles wide. We can and should do the same in Pennsylvania.

Hollidaysburg stands magnificently on a hill between lush pastures and forested mountains.

2. Human scale

The places where we live and work should be built on a people scale rather than a car scale. To give us a feeling of warmth and security, we need communities with sidewalks, lots of street trees, and houses and stores drawn close to the street and to each other. We need places that give us a feeling of belonging and togetherness, not moonscape parking lots and yawning roadways that make anyone not in a car feel alien.

Walking is the best form of exercise and the best way to enjoy the people and the scenery around us. Walking encourages human interaction, which provides most of the joy in our lives and is the lifeblood of our communities.

Obviously, we can't walk everywhere we go, so every neighborhood must make accommodations for the auto. But pedestrians and bicyclists should have equal access to the streets.

There are some buildings — supermarkets, discount warehouses, large manufacturing plants — that require large amounts of parking. But most buildings can be closer together than we currently build them. Even Wal-Marts can be constructed in such a way that nearby residents can walk to them, and their parking lots can be redesigned so they are less forbidding and more pedestrian-friendly.

Marietta's main street is intimate enough to be used for a clogging demonstration during a summertime festival.

78

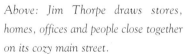

Above: Jim Thorpe draws stores, homes, offices and people close together on its cozy main street.

Right: Residents of Meadville can walk to the library, schools, downtown stores, and this central market.

These homes in Pittsburgh's Shadyside district are part of a self-contained neighborhood.

A Jersey Shore flower store provides a pleasant second floor apartment. Traditional towns mix stores, offices, and residences in the same neighborhoods.

3. Self-contained neighborhoods

Communities should have stores, offices, homes, schools, and parks placed close together. There are thousands of such communities across America, but they were all built prior to World War II. Modern zoning laws require a rigid separation of commercial and residential areas, thus forcing people to drive everywhere.

Let's change these laws to allow pedestrian communities once again. There's no good reason for the separation. The vast majority of offices, stores, restaurants, schools and even light manufacturing plants are compatible with residential neighborhoods.

Americans *will* walk. If they have someplace worth going, the average American will walk ten minutes to get there. That ten-minute walk gives us a radius defining an area of nearly a square mile. That's roughly the size of such beautiful Pennsylvania towns as Jenkintown, Marietta, and Lewisburg.

In towns and neighborhoods of this size, you typically will have enough children to support elementary and secondary schools of 300 to 500 students. That's the optimal size for a school, interestingly enough. Thus, schools can be supported by children living within easy walking distance.

Public safety is increased by mixing uses, because it ensures that neighborhoods remain active throughout the day.

Building close-knit communities with two workplaces for every three dwellings almost guarantees that many residents will find jobs within walking distance. When people live and work in the same area, families benefit by avoiding the need for a second car, and communities benefit by giving people a greater stake in their town's welfare.

Shadyside's main shopping street runs between two residential neighborhoods. Its stores are just a few minutes' walk from hundreds of apartments and single family homes.

4. Diversity

Every Pennsylvania community should include places for people of all ages and incomes to live. Communities should also reflect the racial diversity of the region where they are located.

To make that possible, every neighborhood should provide a wide range of housing types. Small apartment buildings, row houses, small houses on small lots, and large homes can be mixed attractively in the same neighborhoods, making them beautiful as well as practical. Some of the safest and most pleasant communities in Pennsylvania already meet this standard.

Housing elderly people in the same neighborhoods as children means responsible adults will be around during the day to informally look after the neighborhood youngsters. And that gives retirees an enjoyable and vital role to play in the community.

In my town of Pottstown, about ninety seniors volunteer in the classroom annually as part of the school district's Golden Sage program. Seniors can reduce their taxes through a voucher system that pays them for hours spent tutoring school children. But many Pottstown seniors don't do it for the money — they want to be useful and enjoy the invigorating atmosphere of a roomful of children. And the kids desperately need their attention.

Less than 10 percent of all Pennsylvanians are poor. If every neighborhood housed its fair share of the poor, none would be adversely affected by crime or blight. At the same time, wherever our middle class and affluent citizens live, they will automatically contribute to the general welfare. The most important element in a good school system, for example, is a predominance of good students. The most important element in a clean and safe neighborhood is people who take good care of their properties and insist that others do the same.

Reading second-grader Sarah Wildermuth can walk to her grandmother's house by herself after school.

Bethlehem is one of Pennsylvania's healthiest and most beautiful cities. It has housing for people of all ages and incomes, and a resident mix that is about 75 percent non-Hispanic white and 25 percent black, Asian, and Hispanic.

Philadelphia's West Mount Airy
neighborhood has for decades
maintained racial balance and a
high quality housing stock.

Allegheny County was able to retrofit a light rail line through older Pittsburgh suburbs like Dormont because they were originally built with the pedestrian in mind.

The handsome college town of Carlisle has houses, schools, and workplaces placed close enough together to make mass transportation feasible.

5. Transit-friendly design

Every community should provide transportation alternatives for people without cars. Mobility is essential to modern life. No one should be denied that right because they are too young, too old, too poor, or too handicapped to drive a car. One of our greatest problems statewide is the inability of low-income residents to find jobs because they lack transportation.

Trains and buses are far more energy-efficient and far less polluting than cars. They require less space to operate and eliminate the need for parking lots. They encourage public interaction. But public transportation is only feasible when houses and workplaces are concentrated near transit lines.

It's also important to provide bike lanes adjacent to our streets and bike racks at transit stops. A significant percentage of all trips are made by bicycle in most European and Asian countries, and their use is slowly growing in the United States. Bicycles are non-polluting, energy efficient, and take up very little space compared to cars.

The same kind of community design that encourages walking and bicycling helps support mass transit. That's why the "sidewalk" suburbs south of Pittsburgh, built prior to the 1930s, were readily adaptable to a new light rail line Allegheny County built during the 1980s.

All new development should be designed with transit in mind. Even if trains or buses are not immediately practical, they may become so later on. Likewise, new industrial development should be encouraged near rail lines, to encourage more use of trains to carry freight.

Allentown is one of the few communities in Pennsylvania where residents can get where they need to go without a car.

6. Trees

No single element will do more to improve our communities than planting a lot of shade trees. Young trees are inexpensive and require little maintenance. But they grow for decades, developing a beautiful and tranquil presence.

Trees have an enormous calming effect on people. "Why is it I never walk under trees but large and melodious thoughts descend on me?" asked the poet, Walt Whitman. The less romantic people at the journal *Science* published a study that found, over a nine-year period, that surgical patients who could see a cluster of trees outside their windows, instead of brick walls, "had shorter post-operative stays" and "took fewer moderate or strong" painkillers.

Trees counteract the greenhouse effect by absorbing carbon dioxide and releasing oxygen in its place. Their leaves attract and remove dirt, ash, dust, pollen and fumes from the air. Big trees act as powerful air conditioners in the summer and windbreaks in the winter. They soften the landscape, screening eyesores and unifying disparate buildings along the street.

A study by experts from the U. S. Department of Energy, reported in MIT's *Technology Review*, concluded that the most cost-effective way cities can reduce energy consumption is to plant thousands of shade trees and use light-colored materials for roofs and pavement.

The power of trees to enhance our urban areas has been woefully unappreciated. Every parking lot in Pennsylvania should have a minimum of one shade tree for every two parking spaces, evenly distributed throughout the lot. Imagine: Within fifteen years, these lots will look like leafy groves instead of asphalted wastelands. Shade trees should be planted along every street, road, and highway of the Commonwealth, spaced twenty-five to thirty-five feet apart. Walking, bicycling, and even driving will be a pleasure when we surround ourselves with green.

Wyomissing was designed to emphasize trees. Big trees lend an air of elegance and tranquility to every part of the borough.

Meticulously maintained trees help give Wellsboro one of the most pleasing main streets in Pennsylvania.

Above: Tall sycamore trees form an inviting canopy over the main entryway to West Chester.

Left: Every parking lot in Pennsylvania could—and should— look like this one at the Keeneland Association Race Track in Lexington, Ky. Unfortunately, the state called Penn's Woods has nothing like it.

Right: Philadelphia's Chestnut Hill boasts one of the most attractive shopping districts in America.

Below: The secret is to place the parking in back of the stores, not the front. Chestnut Hill parking lots are convenient, and they enjoy a sense of security and enclosure.

Photo © Tom Kelly

Photo © Tom Kelly

7. Alleys and parking lots to the rear

Rare is the householder who puts laundry, cleaning supplies, or household paraphernalia out for guests to see. Yet many homes have ultrawide garage doors and blacktopped areas facing the street, as often as not cluttered with cars, recreational vehicles, and sundry outdoor equipment.

Communities need alleys and rear parking lots to maintain attractive streets and sidewalks.

Just as we, as individuals, have goods and chattel that we put out of sight in closets and storage rooms, we as a community need to set aside things that are not particularly attractive. It is behind our houses that we should put the electric and telephone poles, parking spaces, garages, trash and recycling bins, compost piles, and outdoor equipment. Likewise, parking lots should always be placed to the rear of buildings, or if that is not possible, at the side of buildings. Lots facing the street are a barrier, a visual one to passers-by, a physical one to pedestrians. Parking to the rear can be buffered from adjacent areas and provide a greater sense of enclosure and security.

Alleys are good places to put apartments above garages, fostering a wide range of housing prices in a given neighborhood. A homeowner with a modern day "carriage house" to the rear earns income to help pay the mortgage and provides much better tenant supervision than an absentee landlord. Alleys are also perfect places for older children to play games like basketball. They offer short-cuts to friends' houses. Because they are so closely connected to rear yards, alleys form a semi-private space that residents can share and jointly supervise. If fences, hedges, and trellises are placed tastefully, alleys can also form sheltered pathways for pleasant, quiet ambles.

The best place for cars, outdoor equipment, and garbage cans is in alleys like this one in New Cumberland. This leaves the fronts of homes uncluttered and pedestrian-friendly.

8. Humane architecture

People need to live among buildings that are beautiful and hospitable, and that harmonize with their surroundings. Even as the zoning gurus outlawed traditional communities after World War II, modernist builders rejected traditional architecture, replacing it with steel and glass mutations more appropriate for robots than humans.

We have high schools and public libraries that look more like defensive fortifications than centers of learning. We build hospitals that simulate places of punishment, not temples of healing. We warehouse our elderly in dismal high-rises. We scar open landscapes with monolithic glass towers that loom over meadows and mutilate the sky.

All too often, corporate, civic, and government officials are intimidated by the architectural establishment into approving hideous structures because they are supposedly more functional and state of the art than traditional buildings. Like the loyal subjects in *The Emperor's New Clothes*, these citizens are led to believe only a fool cannot see their merit. The truth is, they have no merit.

There's no reason why our apartment buildings, stores, schools, and offices can't be warm and inviting, constructed using materials and designs that humans have found attractive for generations.

We should also make every effort to preserve our historic buildings. They are a proud part of our heritage, a gift that should be handed down from one generation to the next like a family heirloom.

People love traditional architectural designs — the colonial townhouses of Society Hill, the Gothic villages of England or France, the classical memorials honoring Lincoln and Jefferson in Washington — because they look like they were built for humans, not machines. They give us beauty and a link with the past.

These new rowhomes in Stroudsburg, set close to the sidewalk just a block from the main street, blend the best of the past with the needs of the present.

Below: The Subway Shop in Lewisburg proves that even fast-food restaurants can be attractive.

The new library at Immaculata College, built in 1993, harmonizes beautifully with its surroundings. It has quickly become a much-beloved member of the campus.

Right: Easton's center square, flanked by stores and offices, serves as a splendid focal point for the downtown.

Below: The houses of Delancey Place form a serene outdoor space in the heart of Center City Philadelphia.

9. Outdoor rooms

It is a basic human desire to feel a sense of enclosure. You aren't surprised to hear, for example, that few of us would want a kitchen, living room, or bedroom with the dimensions of a basketball court. But you might be surprised to learn that we want our outdoor living areas to convey a sense of enclosure as well. We treasure places like Harvard Yard, the squares of Savannah, and the plaza at Rockefeller Center because they are such beautifully enclosed spaces.

Out in the suburbs, everything is wide open. The houses, each plunked in the middle of a large lot, not only waste land, they fail to provide any privacy or sense of enclosure. Likewise, they fail to provide any sense of community, because they lack any defined public areas where people can meet and socialize.

Traditional communities like Annapolis or Georgetown, on the other hand, create beautiful outdoor spaces by aligning homes close together to make streets into cozy outdoor rooms. The buildings form the room's walls, while street trees create a cathedral ceiling. Moreover, when homes are placed side-by-side on narrow lots, it is simple to create walled-in back yards that are completely private, easy to maintain, yet large enough for gardens, family gatherings, and romping children.

The land saved can be used to establish parks, within walking distance of every home, that foster a feeling of neighborhood and community. Many Pennsylvania towns — from Lehighton to Meadville — have been designed around public squares that have been used and loved for generations.

Closely spaced houses make possible this lovely courtyard in midtown Harrisburg.

10. Maintenance and safety

Maintenance and safety is the chief difference in appearance between some of Pennsylvania's most fashionable addresses and some of its worst slums. Philadelphia's Germantown and Logan sections, for example, are equal in design, layout, and quality of construction to exclusive residential suburbs like Haverford and Merion. But these Philadelphia neighborhoods are disintegrating for lack of maintenance. Lawns are unkempt, alleys overflow with trash, abandoned cars dot the streets. Crime is a constant fear.

If Philadelphia was not overloaded with the poor and troubled, the city could be among the world's most desirable places to live. It is not the physical design of cities like Philadelphia, Reading, and Harrisburg that is the problem. It is their eroding and dangerous neighborhoods that drive people away. Pervasive trash, deteriorated buildings, and graffiti go hand-in-hand with soaring crime rates.

Improved policing methods can dramatically lower crime rates. In New York City, for example, aggressive policing strategies have helped reduce crime to the city's lowest level in 30 years.

Rigorous attention to maintenance is also essential. To prevent neighborhood deterioration from getting out of control, local government must:

- Implement a comprehensive street cleaning program.
- Prevent junk from accumulating on private property by cleaning it up and placing a lien on the property to eventually recover the cost.
- Inventory all properties and ensure code inspections are done regularly — perhaps on a five-year cycle.
- Create a user-friendly system to issue building and licensing permits.
- Use the discretion allowed in Pennsylvania's uniform construction code to encourage the restoration of older buildings.
- Streamline procedures to facilitate the sale of abandoned properties to new owners who will restore or redevelop them.

Some of the best-built housing in Pennsylvania is located in its worst neighborhoods. Maintenance makes the difference.

Left: The Georgetown section of Washington, D.C., just a short walk from Georgetown University, is one of America's most exclusive neighborhoods. The quality of its homes is no different from homes in some of Philadelphia's worst neighborhoods. Maintenance makes the difference.

Below: A once-fabulous row of houses in Philadelphia, now falling apart, is located just a short walk from Temple University and Broad Street, one of the city's main commercial streets. Overwhelmed by social problems, the city failed to act promptly at the first sign of decline to prevent the deterioration and widespread abandonment of the neighborhood.

Lessons for Pennsylvania

Many creative communities, including a dozen states, are coming to grips with the problems and opportunities I've sketched out thus far. After extensive research and much discussion, these communities have formulated long-range strategies, based on the principles of smart growth, to preserve their environment and create quality communities. They have faced dissension, distractions, and numerous setbacks along the way. But they have persevered. They have articulated their goals, laid their plans, and started to adopt the laws necessary to achieve their goals.

Pennsylvania can — and must — profit from their example.

Saving farms and towns with growth boundaries

Oregon is twice as big as Pennsylvania, but it has only a fourth as many people. "There's plenty of room!" one would think. "Sprawl's a non-issue!"

But the typical Oregon resident lives in an urban area, on a much smaller lot than those typically found in Pennsylvania suburbs.

It's not that Oregonians don't love the countryside. They do. That's why they've declared it off limits to sprawling development.

Unlike Pennsylvania, Oregon's primary unit of local government is the city, which ranges in size from Portland, the state's largest municipality, down to tiny Greenhorn, with a population of just three. In 1973, the Oregon Legislature passed the most comprehensive land-use law in the country. Each of the state's 242 cities and 36 counties was required to adopt comprehensive plans and zoning laws in accordance with state goals. The process took more than ten years.

The key element in Oregon's land-use system is the urban growth boundary. Each of Oregon's cities has drawn a line around itself that encompasses the existing buildings and infrastructure, along with enough vacant land to accommodate development for a twenty-year period. Virtually all development must take place within that boundary. Land outside the boundary is reserved for farm and forest use.

Oregon has found the best way to protect its farms and forests is to concentrate development in its cities, like Portland, assuring they remain safe and pleasant places to live.

Photo © Falconer/West Stock

The change has been dramatic. Before the boundaries were drawn, Oregon's prime farming area, the Willamette Valley, was zoned for residential lots. Now, 16 million acres of farmland are reserved exclusively for agriculture. Nine million acres are zoned only for forestry uses. Fewer than 3 million acres are open to development. "Oregon has had more success in protecting agricultural land through a balanced system of planning, land use, and growth management controls than any other state," says Dr. John DeGrove, a national expert on land-use planning.

"We've been strong supporters of the law ever since the concept was proposed," says Philip Fell, longtime spokesman for the Oregon League of Cities. "We want to prevent urban sprawl, and we want to allow development in an orderly way to reduce the cost of providing services." Although the law was originally intended to protect farmland and the environment, the protection of Oregon's cities has proved an equally important benefit, he says. Developers support urban growth boundaries because they provide certainty that their projects will be approved without costly delays and court battles.

Oregon residents are more willing to live in cities and towns because they recognize that's the best way to protect Oregon's open spaces, says Mitch Rohse, president of Oregon's planning association. "I think the ethos or culture of land-use planning has absolutely permeated the population," he says. "A lot of people here are migrants from other states. They came to enjoy fishing and hiking and all the amenities Oregon has to offer, and they want to save them."

In New Brunswick, N.J., new townhouses have been built within walking distance of Johnson & Johnson's world headquarters, the white skyscraper in the background.

New Jersey's state plan requires all state agencies to encourage development in the state's cities and towns. The village of Cranbury represents the kind of pedestrian community New Jersey hopes to encourage throughout the state.

Reviving traditional communities

In 1992, after six years of study and debate, New Jersey adopted a statewide comprehensive plan designed to revive its troubled cities, encourage traditional communities similar to Princeton and Cape May, and save farms and open space by curbing sprawl.

In the past, says former Rutgers University professor Mark Lapping, "Planning was a piece here, a bit there, a space there. And when you added it all up together, the cumulative impact was the nickel and diming to death of the New Jersey landscape and the New Jersey quality of life."

Working with local municipalities, the state first identified more than 600 "centers," ranging in size from cities like Newark and Trenton to hamlets designed for no more than 250 residents. Local municipalities were encouraged to draw "community development boundaries" around these centers showing the maximum area that will eventually be developed. Traditional, town-like development with a mixture of houses, offices, and stores is envisioned inside the centers. Only very rural development is desired outside the boundaries.

New offices and stores enhance Princeton's Palmer Square.

Before adopting this plan, the New Jersey Legislature required an independent assessment of its likely impact. A year-long study directed by Rutgers University concluded that implementing the plan would save the government up to $1.3 billion in infrastructure costs over a twenty-year period and another $400 million annually in operating costs.

To help revive its cities, New Jersey changed its building code in 1998 to make it easier to rehabilitate older structures. Within a year, investment in older buildings increased 60 percent.

In 1999, the legislature authorized $1 billion in bonds to preserve one million acres of farmland and open space over the next ten years — half the undeveloped land remaining in New Jersey. "We must find the will to stop development that costs more than it saves, takes more than it gives, and that diminishes our lives and degrades our surroundings," says Gov. James McGreevey.

During a ten-year period, with input from local municipalities, the state Office of Smart Growth developed a statewide map showing where development will be encouraged and where it will be restricted. After adjustments are made to the map by the state Department of Environmental Protection, reflecting natural resource data, the map will be used by the state government to guide state funding and permitting for new projects.

Right now, people don't have choices about where they want to live, says Barbara Lawrence, director of New Jersey Future, a citizens' group formed to promote the plan. "Today, if you want to live in a nice house and send your kids to a nice school, you have to live in a classic suburban house on a cul-de-sac and drive everywhere, even for a quart of milk. The state plan is about giving people a choice to live in a town where the streets are safe and the schools are good."

Washington officials believe that building town-like communities is the best method to preserve the state's farmland.

Stressing town-like development

Washington state boasts nearly every kind of scenery the West has to offer, from snow-capped mountains to pristine forests and endless miles of prairie. Thanks to an economy as diverse as its topography, Washington has become one of the nation's most popular destinations in recent decades, growing eight times faster than Pennsylvania since 1950.

To prevent the erosion of its natural resources and quality of life, Washington adopted in the early 1990s a far-reaching series of laws to curb suburban sprawl and concentrate growth in its cities. "A lot of people in this part of the world are from somewhere else," says state official Joe Tovar. "They really treasure the environment they've found here. They don't

Washington's state planning process, begun in 1991, encourages people to live in the kind of close-knit neighborhoods typical of Seattle.

want to repeat the mistakes other places have made." The new laws require counties to establish urban growth boundaries around Washington cities that will contain all projected growth for the next twenty years. Land outside these urban growth areas will be preserved for farming, forestry, or as open space.

In the future, housing should be constructed on smaller lots and placed closer to stores and offices, so people can walk to work or take mass transit, says attorney Richard Ford, who helped write the planning laws. That will reduce the cost of housing and infrastructure like water and sewer lines, reduce traffic on the highways, protect farms and forests, and improve everyone's quality of life.

"We have to return to the form of neighborhood closer to what we had a century ago," says Seattle architect Mark Hinshaw. "We need more three- and four-story housing, and a higher quality of design to make sure new buildings fit in with existing neighborhoods. We need the return of the corner store, and more parks for children. It can mean quite wonderful, close-knit communities." Under the growth management laws, Washington counties and cities must also agree to accept their fair share of low- and moderate-income housing.

Most city and county officials believe the new system will help create healthy communities and preserve Washington's natural resources for generations to come.

"For the first time, cities and counties are sitting down at the same table, sharing information and working together," says David Williams, of the Association of Washington Cities. "We have a lot of communities doing the 'visioning thing,' with people literally identifying what they like and don't like about their communities, what they want their communities to be in the future. It's a healthy process."

Protecting a village-centered way of life

Marcy Harding, a banker, state official, and conservationist, has lived all of her fifty-four years in Vermont. "I love Vermont's rural character," she says. "We still have tight-knit little villages where there is a strong sense of community. I like the fact you can drive through farmland and see it's still being worked."

Although Vermont is a fifth of the size of Pennsylvania, it has only about as many people — 609,000 — as Bucks County. It is one of the most rural states in the nation, with most people living in villages or along country roads.

Like many Vermonters, Harding used to take the villages and open space for granted. But in the mid 1980s, a residential building boom engulfed the state. Vermont's scenic beauty, together with its improved access from New York and Boston via interstate highways, attracted wealthy out-of-staters looking for vacation homes.

"Vermont was being carved up," says Mark Snelling, son of the late governor Richard Snelling. Residents were concerned about the loss of farmland, the rising cost of housing, and sprawling housing patterns that threatened to obliterate the distinctive look of Vermont villages and surrounding countryside. Snelling was named to a governor's Commission on Vermont's Future to study land-use issues, conduct public hearings across the state, and recommend new legislation.

As a result of the commission's recommendations, Vermont passed a growth management measure, Act 200, establishing twelve statewide planning goals. Chief among the goals is "to plan development so as to maintain the historic settlement pattern of compact village and urban centers separated by rural countryside."

To do that, Vermont relies heavily on a law called Act 250, which establishes criteria to ensure that new development does not detract from existing town centers. For example, the state succeeded in persuading retailers like Wal-Mart to locate in existing vacant buildings in traditional towns like Rutland and Bennington rather than in "greenfield" sites outside of town.

In 1998, Vermont increased the proportion of state funding for local schools from 30 percent to 72 percent, which reduced pressure on towns to chase after new development just to increase their tax base.

A downtown bill provides incentives for developers to rehabilitate buildings, including upper stories, in traditional downtowns and village centers.

With the help of citizen volunteer Marcy Harding, the town of Richmond had its plan approved by the regional planning commission and adopted by the townspeople. "We increased the density of development in the village center so it will continue the pattern of the original town," she says.

The state's business community supports such measures, says John Ewing, retired president of the Bank of Vermont. "The consensus is that the planning effort of Act 200 is good for the state."

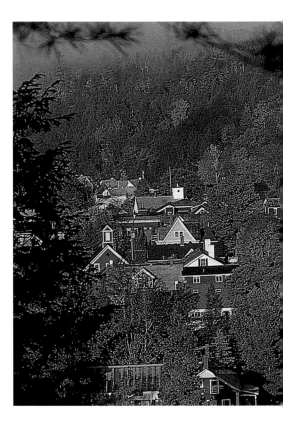

The state plan is designed to preserve the integrity of lovely villages like Stowe.

The Vermont state plan, adopted in 1988, encourages development that maintains Vermont's historic settlement patterns of compact villages surrounded by open space. Marcy Harding and Gary Bressor of the Richmond Land Trust believe the state plan can help protect their town of Richmond.

Photo © Paul O. Boisvert

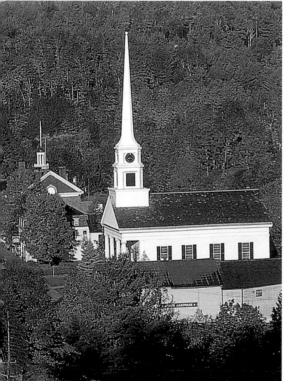

The Underhill Center Post Office typifies Vermont's village ambience.

Save the Chesapeake, protect Delaware

Maryland's Chesapeake Bay, the largest and most productive estuary in the United States, is one of the ecological wonders of the world. But it may not be much longer.

"The Chesapeake Bay is balanced on a knife-edge of survival," wrote Michael Barnes, chairman of a 1990 panel studying the future of the Chesapeake Bay region. "There is no doubt that unmanaged growth, suburban sprawl, and the destruction of forest land and farmland will kill the bay."

To help save the Chesapeake, Maryland's General Assembly passed a statewide planning act in 1992 to change land use patterns in the state. The law was strengthened in 1997 to require all counties to identify "smart growth" areas where development makes the most sense. The state will only fund roads, water and sewer systems, economic development and housing projects in those areas.

In essence, Maryland wants new homes and offices to be built on smaller lots, closer together, and concentrated in and around existing developed areas. In rural areas, the state wants development concentrated in specially designated growth centers.

"If smart growth is going to work, it's not just about restraining sprawl elsewhere, but making existing communities viable," says Parris Glendening, who popularized the term "smart growth" as Maryland's governor from 1995 to 2002. "If we can help those communities blossom, the whole state will blossom."

Maryland developers are willing to recreate small town-type environments, says Kay Bienen, who worked on the legislation for the Maryland Homebuilders Association. "A lot of it is getting people to accept changes," she says. "They need to be shown you can live in a private setting and don't need five acres to do it."

In 1995, with the passage of the "Shaping Delaware's Future Act," Delaware joined the growing movement to enact comprehensive planning legislation. Delaware's new law required the state's municipalities to adopt new comprehensive plans in accordance with ten state goals. The goals include redeveloping existing communities rather than consuming more farmland and open space; making older communities more attractive; and providing alternatives to the car for people to get around.

New state initiatives range from grants for redeveloping abandoned industrial lands to impact fees levied on development sited in rural areas.

Delaware's three counties have adopted state-approved plans, and 90 percent of the state's local municipalities have plans that are either state-certified or under review.

Immediately after taking office in 2001, Gov. Ruth Ann Minner launched her "Livable Delaware" program to ensure that "counties and municipalities plan where they are going to grow and then only grow where they plan." The state will withhold funding to municipalities that allow low density, sprawling development.

"Livable Delaware sends a clear message," says Gov. Minner. "We value our quality of life here in Delaware, and we will no longer support sprawl with taxpayer's money."

Above: Historic Delaware towns like New Castle contain the convenient mixture of stores, homes, and offices the state hopes to encourage in new development.

Left: Maryland initially began its comprehensive state planning process to protect its most important natural resource, the Chesapeake Bay.

Right: Lexington, Kentucky, created the nation's first urban growth boundary during the 1950s to preserve its gorgeous Bluegrass country. The boundary has helped keep the city of Lexington healthy.

Below: The boundary has protected Lexington's world-famous horse farms from sprawling development.

Preserving the Bluegrass country

The Bluegrass region surrounding Lexington, Kentucky, is one of the most beautiful places on earth.

Horses frolic on manicured pastureland, carefully framed by endless lines of white or black plank fences. Narrow country roads meander through rolling countryside unspoiled by the passage of time. Handsome mansions and ornate barns, placed amid groves of oak or ash, complete the storybook picture of perfection.

That so much beauty has been spared from strip development and housing tracts is little short of miraculous. It's the result of good planning.

"We cannot afford to let the development of this region to chance," says Robert Clay, owner of Three Chimneys horse farm. "Selling out in the short term and ruining the landscape is not in our long-term economic interests," adds Buck Woodford, president of the Kentucky Bank.

The Lexington area is protected by a unique city-county government and the nation's first urban growth boundary. Lexington formed a joint planning commission with Fayette County in 1928 and established an urban growth boundary in 1958. The city and county merged governments in 1974.

The growth boundary, which has been adjusted several times in the last forty years, delineates where development will and will not be permitted. All urban development is contained within the boundary; only rural uses, with a minimum lot size of forty acres, are permitted outside the boundary.

To permanently protect its farmland, the county created a purchase of development rights program in 2000 to preserve 50,000 acres of rural Fayette County during the next twenty years.

Thanks to these policies, 93 percent of the county's 225,000 residents live within the urban growth boundary. The rural service zone, containing 70 percent of Lexington-Fayette's land area, is virtually unspoiled.

Unlike Pennsylvania, where many single family homes are built on lots of an acre or more, the typical lot size in Lexington-Fayette is a quarter to a sixth of an acre.

Alex Warren, a retired business executive who headed Toyota's American operations in nearby Georgetown, says Kentucky's rural scenery is vital to the region's prosperity.

"From a business standpoint, the quality of life is the key to our national reputation and image," he says. "We are known for our beautiful landscapes filled with horse farms and green grass. We've got to make sure those elements continue to exist."

Nine of ten county residents live within the boundary (in blue) leaving 70 percent of Lexington-Fayette County unspoiled.

Investing in open space

If you like mountains, fast-flowing streams, and every kind of outdoor recreation, you'll like Boulder, Colorado. If you like book stores, fine shops, and cultural events, you'll like Boulder.

Boulder has the best of both worlds: all the amenities of a city and all the open space of the West.

With 100,000 residents living on twenty-seven square miles, Boulder is slightly larger than Scranton in size and population.

Unlike Scranton and every other Pennsylvania city, Boulder is surrounded by a sixty-eight square mile "greenbelt" of public open space and mountain parks — an area much larger than the city itself. Boulder owns another 2,156 acres of parks within city limits.

Running through Boulder is an eleven-mile greenway system along seven creeks and several major thoroughfares. It forms a secondary transportation corridor for pedestrians, bicyclists, and skaters.

For Boulder residents, three-quarters of whom work in town, biking can be faster than driving. "An awful lot of people ride bikes as their main form of transportation," says John Lowe, an engineer.

Boulder's superb park and open space system is a direct result of environmentally conscious residents. The greenbelt idea, for example, was proposed by two University of Colorado professors who were appalled by a housing development creeping up the mountains. They proposed, and city residents approved by referendum in 1959, a "blue line" ordinance that prohibits any development more than 400 feet above the city's elevation of 5,350 feet.

To prevent suburban sprawl, city voters approved a one-cent sales tax in 1967, dedicating 40 percent of the revenues to open space acquisition. In 1989, voters approved an additional third of a cent sales tax for open space. The tax has generated more than $160 million to buy ranchland and conservation easements.

The city directly controls about two-thirds of the land extending four to five miles outside its borders, and the rest is unlikely to be developed. In Boulder County, no land can be subdivided to more than two units per thirty-five-acre parcel unless it is provided with city services. Boulder refuses to provide services beyond city limits.

Because of these restrictions, Boulder County has retained the rural character of land surrounding the city, and the city's land purchase program assures Boulder will be permanently surrounded by open space.

Boulder has a population density similar to Pennsylvania cities like Scranton, Bethlehem, and Williamsport. Yet no one feels cooped in, says former councilman Steve Pomerance, because open space is so easily accessible. "Boulder's a nice place, and it will become more attractive in the future," he says. "I don't know what's keeping other cities from doing the same thing."

Boulder is surrounded by a 42,700-acre "greenbelt" that includes part of the Flatiron Mountains.

Right: Oak Park is one of the loveliest communities in America. For thirty years, the village has strived to maintain racial diversity and a high quality of life for all its citizens.

Above: The village has housing of every kind. It is all meticulously maintained.

Right: Roberta Raymond and Angela Collins-Woods of the Oak Park Regional Housing Center, which promotes racial integration.

Integrating the community

Oak Park, Illinois, adjacent to Chicago's west side, is one of America's loveliest communities. The home of Frank Lloyd Wright and some of his finest architecture, the village of 53,000 is a tranquil blend of quiet streets, huge trees, handsome houses, elegant apartment buildings, and carefully tended lawns.

Neither architecture nor beauty, however, makes Oak Park the special place it is. Thanks to careful planning, Oak Park is a racially and economically integrated community. During the last thirty years, the village has seen its black population increase from virtually zero to 22 percent. At the same time, it has maintained housing prices well above the regional average. Although the typical Oak Park homeowner is a professional or executive, nearly a quarter of Oak Park's residents have low or moderate incomes.

"Oak Park's reputation for diversity wasn't easy to come by," says planner William Merrill, a thirty-five year resident of the village. In 1968, after a bitter political struggle, Oak Park trustees passed one of the first fair housing laws in the country and later developed the village's first comprehensive plan to foster positive change. The plan emphasized three areas: quality housing, economic development, and racial diversity.

In 1972, the Oak Park Regional Housing Center was established as a non-profit, village-funded housing agency whose sole mission was to promote racial integration in Oak Park. The key to maintaining an integrated community, says Roberta L. Raymond, founder of the center, is to not only welcome blacks but ensure white demand remains high. "If white demand does not continue in a neighborhood, then when whites leave for natural reasons — new jobs, death, divorce — and no new whites take their place, the community resegregates to all black," she says. The housing center advertises in both national and Chicago-area magazines, promoting Oak Park as a fine place to live. It works with regional employers such as hospitals and corporations to encourage people to live in Oak Park. The center has become regional, opening an office in a suburb several miles west of Oak Park. "From a planning perspective, we have to be regional," Raymond says. "Oak Park can't be the only shining beacon to which every minority is attracted, or we'll resegregate."

Oak Park has a rigorous code inspection program. The exterior and common areas of all multi-family buildings are inspected annually, as are the interiors of 10 percent of all rental units. Whenever an apartment building is sold, the property is inspected inside and out.

Another non-profit corporation, the Oak Park Residence Corporation, buys, rehabilitates, and manages apartment buildings in the town.

"Oak Park felt it needed an independent arm to deal with blight wherever it was located," says Frank Muriello, longtime director of the Corporation. "When we acquire a building, we usually over-improve it, primarily to create white demand. We want to have the best buildings in town." Whenever the Residence Corporation acquires a building or takes over its management, it takes steps to integrate the building. Oak Park discourages apartment buildings that are either all-white or all-black.

During the last thirty-five years, the Residence Corporation has rehabilitated about twenty-five multi-family buildings. It currently owns and manages fifteen buildings with 360 dwelling units. The Residence Corporation also performs other community maintenance work. "You don't see any houses boarded up in Oak Park," Muriello says. "That's the worst thing that can happen to a neighborhood."

The village boasts 120 volunteer gardeners who plant and maintain flower beds all over town. "Oak Park has more citizen participation than any place I've ever seen," says Gary Schwab, chairman of the beautification committee.

Oak Park has not achieved full integration, says Robert Sherrell, a black who served four years as village trustee. Sherrell's two children, for example, found that blacks and whites felt pressure to segregate themselves when they got to high school. But the village is still way ahead of the rest of the nation. "It's a struggle," Sherrell says. "Oak Park didn't decide it wanted to be something without a lot of work. It works because everyone works at it."

Housing center founder Raymond, who has lived in Oak Park most of her life, says life in Oak Park has never been better. "A different kind of social phenomenon takes place in communities that have sidewalks and cultural richness within walking distance," she says. "From my house I can walk to a multitude of restaurants, a wonderful library, different cultural events, two major shopping districts, ballet classes and an art school. When people can walk, they view their community differently. You can see more, appreciate the gardens. You stop to talk to people. The whole sense of neighborhood is different. To me, this is the community of the future, the way people should be living."

Oak Park may be the best known, perhaps, but it is not the only community that has made racial integration succeed. Across the country, you can find others that are doing it.

Shaker Heights, an affluent streetcar suburb immediately adjacent to predominately black neighborhoods of Cleveland, Ohio, decided in the early 1960s that it would actively try to create and maintain a racially balanced community. Among its innovative programs are low-cost loans to whites who move into black areas and blacks who move into white areas. During the past thirty years, Shaker Heights' black population has slowly grown to about a third of the community, even as property values have risen faster than the regional average for Cleveland suburbs. The state of Ohio also has encouraged integration by offering low interest loans to whites who buy homes in predominately black neighborhoods and blacks who move into mostly white neighborhoods.

In Denver, scores of poor families live in homes scattered throughout working- and middle-class neighborhoods of the city. It's a result of the city's policy of dispersing public housing in single units. In 2002, Denver City Council passed an ordinance requiring all developments of thirty or more for-sale units to set aside 10 percent of the units for low and moderate-income people.

Inclusionary housing is a great idea, says Dottie Rees, a twenty-five-year resident of Denver's Park Hill neighborhood. Rees notes with pride that both a poor family and a justice of the Colorado Supreme Court live on her block. "We want and nurture diversity," she says. "My children were raised to appreciate people from all different backgrounds. That's the greatest education you can give a child."

Park Hill is one of numerous racially integrated neighborhoods that have remained safe, attractive, and stable over a period of thirty years, such as Butler-Tarkington in Indianapolis, Ind.; Belmont-Hillsboro in Nashville, Tenn.; and West Mount Airy in Philadelphia.

Blair Seitz, the photographer for this book, and I know that racially and economically integrated communities can work, because we live in them. Blair and his wife live in an integrated neighborhood of Harrisburg. My wife and I love living in the heart of a real town — Pottstown.

From the back door of our house to the newspaper where I worked for twenty-two years is a two-minute walk. My wife can walk to her elementary school in fifteen minutes. By not having to commute a half-hour to work every day, we've saved ourselves about 13,500 hours behind the wheel during the last three decades — the equivalent of seven years at work. And we've saved about $200,000 in transportation costs. We have a car — we like our car — but it's our servant, not our master.

My house is on a tenth of an acre lot. I have a little spot next to the house for our car, and a yard that's private and big enough for our dog and family gatherings, with mature trees and shrubbery — birds, squirrels, even an occasional possum.

I live in an integrated neighborhood that closely mirrors the racial diversity of our state. It's a low- and moderate-income neighborhood, but it's still pleasant because of the critical mass factor. We have a predominant number of people who take good care of their properties and they set the tone for everyone else. In the last fifteen years, we've brought new industry into our town, planted more than 2,000 street trees, created two historic districts, and seen the restoration of numerous homes and commercial buildings. If Pottstown had more middle class families to add to the mix, and restored train service to Philadelphia and Reading, I could hardly imagine a better place to live.

My home town of Pottstown is an excellent walking town. Right, my wife's second graders stop in our back yard to pet our dog, Rugby, on a walking trip to the Phillies Fire Co. and the Pottstown Police Department.

Above: Thanks to a regional government and tax base sharing, Minneapolis is one of the healthiest cities in America.

Right: Metropolitan Portland, Oregon, keeps development within a 397-square-mile urban growth boundary. Land outside the boundary is reserved for farms and forests.

Governing on a regional basis

The problems of poverty, crime, and race will never be solved until governments act regionally. That's the judgment of urban policy expert David Rusk. Older cities like Philadelphia, Pittsburgh, and Harrisburg are struggling under an immense burden: they are the regional warehouses for Pennsylvania's poor. None can remain viable without involving their entire metropolitan regions. "In America, 'the city' has been redefined since World War II," Rusk says. "The real city is now the whole metropolitan area."

Studies by economist Richard Voith of the Federal Reserve Board show that the fate of cities and their suburbs are linked. Looking at the economic performance of twenty-eight metropolitan areas in the Northeast and Midwest, Voith concluded the suburbs of economically healthy cities did better than the suburbs of ailing cities.

Reflecting that reality, states like North Carolina allow cities to annex adjacent developing suburbs, without any referendums. Raleigh, Durham, and Charlotte, for example, have regularly expanded in recent decades. "We don't have the situation of rich incorporated suburbs that have made themselves enclaves of wealthy white people who spend all their tax money in their own area," says David Godschalk, professor at the University of North Carolina. "Our cities have been able to annex and grow and keep the suburbs as part of their tax base. And they keep suburbanites as part of the civic culture in the cities, so you don't lose all that leadership."

Going beyond annexation, Minnesota and Oregon have created metropolitan governments.

The Twin Cities Metropolitan Council provides regional services in a seven-county area surrounding Minneapolis-St. Paul, including mass transportation, a regional water and sewer system, an airport authority, and a regional parks system. Municipalities within the Metro Council region also share their local tax base according to population and need. Although the region's wealthiest municipality has fifty times more commercial/industrial property per resident than the poorest municipality, the tax base disparity has been reduced to just twelve to one because of tax base sharing.

Oregon's Portland Metropolitan Service District, which covers three counties and twenty-four cities, is the only popularly elected regional government in America. Metro runs a regional park system, including the Metro zoo, a regional water and sewer system, a regional trash system, and a regional convention complex.

But Metro's most important function is controlling development, which is confined within an urban growth boundary covering 397 square miles. Most land outside the boundary is strictly reserved for agriculture and forestry uses. Metro decides when and if the boundary should be expanded. It decides the location of new light rail lines, highways, and regional facilities like shopping centers and industrial parks. To help create more affordable housing and disperse it throughout the region, Metro requires all its municipalities to zone housing at an average density ranging from six to ten units per acre. Says former Mayor Gussie McRobert of Gresham, one of Metro's fastest growing cities: "In Oregon we have a tradition of being able to set aside our individual interest for the broader good of the community."

Photo © Jeff Gnass/West Stock

The safe city

Like Philadelphia and Pittsburgh, Toronto boasts gleaming skyscrapers, indoor shopping malls, and ethnic diversity. When it comes to cleanliness and public safety, however, Toronto is in a class by itself.

Toronto's commercial streets are washed daily and its residential streets cleaned weekly. While Toronto is an ethnically diverse city — half its residents were born outside Canada — it has nothing like America's dangerous, decayed ghettos. Its murder rate, for example, is one-tenth that of Philadelphia. According to the *Places Rated Almanac*, Toronto is North America's safest big city.

"Toronto and other Canadian cities are fundamentally different from American cities in two ways," says John Sewell, former mayor of Toronto. "They're denser, and the incomes of the residents are far more mixed. We take it for granted that people of all incomes live together in all sorts of neighborhoods." While older American cities lost their middle class to the suburbs in the decades following World War II, Toronto didn't. "Americans got this idea of suburbs where you have communities of all one income group," Sewell says. "In Toronto, that idea was buried by the planners, who put all kinds of housing types in the suburbs and attracted a wide variety of people." To keep a healthy balance of residents, the provincial government of Ontario requires 30 percent of all new housing in every municipality to be affordable to low- and moderate-income residents.

The city also profited from a regional government called Metro Toronto, created in 1953. In Pennsylvania, each city, township and borough draws up its own comprehensive plan, which includes zoning for every conceivable land use. There is no coordination in the siting of highways, water and sewer lines, malls, office parks, or anything else that affects people on a regional basis. Metro Toronto did it the other way around. In cooperation with its six member municipalities, the Metro government drew up a master plan showing where major highways and mass transit lines would go, and where housing, offices, and manufacturing would be encouraged. As a result, 34 percent of all work trips in Toronto are made by mass transit and another 6 percent of its residents walk to their jobs.

Pleased with the success of Metro Toronto, the provincial government of Ontario merged the six municipalities of Metro Toronto into the City of Toronto in January 1998.

Toronto's planning department expects 540,000 new residents and an equal number of new jobs in the next thirty years. But the city hopes to attract up to a million new residents during that time, without building a phalanx of skyscrapers. The secret, planners say, is to transform abandoned industrial tracts, warehouse districts, and underused parcels into neighborhoods that are close to public transportation and contain both jobs and housing. "Having more jobs next to homes doesn't guarantee people will live and work in the same neighborhood, but it does offer more choices," says planner Brenda Bernards. "It makes better use of our infrastructure and creates a more balanced community."

Above: Former mayor John Sewell rides his bike to work in good weather.

Right: Walking, bicycling, and riding the trolley are a way of life in Toronto.

Left: Mass transit, not the private car, is the nucleus of Toronto's transportation system.

Below: 'Madvacs' clean the sidewalks daily in commercial areas.

Recycling land in our cities and towns

Like Toronto, Pennsylvania cities also have the capacity to accommodate thousands of new residents and jobs by redeveloping abandoned industrial tracts and other vacant or underused parcels of land.

For example. Herr's Island, directly across the Allegheny River from Pittsburgh's Golden Triangle, was for years derelict and polluted, the site of an abandoned meat packing plant and scrap yard.

"Debris, junked cars, buses, trucks — infested with rats — the place was terrible," said Don Montgomery, an architect and developer. "Just to clean up the debris seemed overwhelming."

But with the help of the city and the state, Montgomery and his colleagues transformed the forty-three-acre island into one of the most fashionable residential and office complexes in Pennsylvania. Now called Washington's Landing, the site boasts eighty-eight upscale townhouses with panoramic views of Pittsburgh's skyline, office buildings, tennis courts, a marina, and a lovely park that's linked to a greenway along the banks of the Allegheny River.

For years, federal environmental laws made industrial ruins like Herr's Island off-limits to business and industry. The laws required that "brownfields" — vacant industrial lands — be cleaned up to "Garden of Eden" standards at the expense of anyone and everyone who had anything to do with the property. Unfortunately, the laws generated millions of dollars in lawsuits but very little environmental improvement. Instead, they virtually guaranteed that thousands of acres of vacant land in our cities and towns remained eyesores while developers plowed over cornfields and woodlands for new homes, stores, and offices.

Frustrated with the inability of his hometown of Lebanon to do anything with an abandoned steel plant in its midst, state Sen. David Brightbill introduced legislation to make it easier to reuse brownfields in Pennsylvania. Signed by Gov. Ridge as the Land Recycling Act of 1995, the law gives the state Department of Environmental Protection discretion to approve flexible clean-up standards for previously developed land, depending on the proposed new use of the land. Meanwhile, the federal Environmental Protection Agency agreed it would not challenge the state's decision to approve specific site clean-ups.

At Herr's Island, using discretion meant that when PCBs, a suspected carcinogen, were found at the site, the developers were allowed to find creative solutions to the problem. (The PCBs were sealed in a rubber liner under the tennis courts.)

Since the program's inception, 1,350 brownfield sites from Erie to Philadelphia have been cleaned up and returned to productive use, and hundreds more are in the pipeline. The potential to rebuild our cities is enormous: There are more than 50,000 abandoned buildings and empty lots in Philadelphia, about 15,000 vacant tracts in Pittsburgh, and thousands more in smaller cities and towns that could be recycled.

The state Department of Environmental Protection

Above: Herr's Island in Pittsburgh was vacant for years, the site of an old scrap yard and abandoned meat packing plant.

Right: The island has been cleaned up and transformed into a lovely residential and office development with a restaurant, marina, and a park connected to a greenway along the Allegheny River.

is providing grants to local municipalities to inventory brownfield sites in Pennsylvania for inclusion in a statewide website listing. In addition, the state is putting together marketing and financial resources to maximize each property's redevelopment potential.

"The idea behind land recycling is not simply to encourage development," Sen. Brightbill says. "Development is going to happen anyway. This program is designed to encourage development that will revive neighborhoods, bring jobs back to our cities, and make the best use of our land."

Photo © Michael Haritan

Lancaster is working to preserve its unique way of life.

Above: Lancaster County's plan for growth boundaries should help preserve its city and boroughs and protect the farmland surrounding them.

Left: The city of Lancaster will become a focal point for new development.

Back to the future

Since 1980, Lancaster County has been the fastest growing metropolitan area in Pennsylvania. Although residents are pleased with the prosperity that growth brings, they realize sprawling development is destroying the very qualities that make Lancaster the uniquely beautiful place it is.

After several years of soul-searching and debate, a coalition of businessmen, developers, farmers, and environmentalists endorsed a bold new plan in 1993 to protect the county's farmland, revive the City of Lancaster, and restore Lancaster's historic town-centered pattern of development.

"Lancaster County in the 1980s grew by just about the same population — 60,000 residents — as the city of Lancaster contains," says Lancaster planning director Ronald Bailey. "The difference is the city of Lancaster takes up about 7.2 square miles, while in the 1980s we converted somewhere between 60 and 70 square miles of agricultural land to accommodate the same number of people."

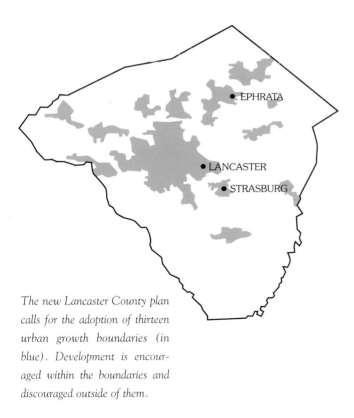

The new Lancaster County plan calls for the adoption of thirteen urban growth boundaries (in blue). Development is encouraged within the boundaries and discouraged outside of them.

By shaping new development in the form of traditional, compact communities, where homes, offices and schools are close enough so people can walk to some of their activities, Lancaster can preserve virtually all its prime farmland, Bailey says.

Using a computerized map called a geographic information system, the Lancaster County Planning Commission designated thirteen urban growth areas centered around the city of Lancaster and boroughs like Ephrata, Lititz, Mt. Joy, and Columbia.

These areas contain sufficient land to accommodate all the commercial, industrial, and residential growth expected during the next twenty years, plus an extra margin of 50 percent. Future development is encouraged within the growth areas and discouraged outside of them. The redevelopment of vacant and underutilized land in older urban areas, such as the city of Lancaster, is strongly advocated.

Forty-four of the county's sixty municipalities have cooperated in implementing the growth areas. At the same time, the county has prepared model ordinances for its municipalities that foster traditional, pedestrian-oriented communities.

The results have been dramatic. By the mid 1990s, the rate of land consumed for development dropped by more than half. Thanks to an aggressive farmland preservation program, for every acre developed, three acres were permanently preserved. About 65 percent of the county is still being used for agriculture.

"We believe urban growth boundaries can work," says Scott Jackson, former director of the Lancaster Building Industries Association.

Janet Milkman, president of 10,000 Friends of Pennsylvania, believes Lancaster County can help provide a model for the state. "Pennsylvania's land-use authority is fragmented among thousands of local municipalities, state and county agencies, and special districts," she says. "We must get our act together and make the 'big picture' decisions about where we want growth according to a county or regional plan. Otherwise, we will continue to destroy both our cities and our countryside."

Framing a Plan for Pennsylvania

A comprehensive state plan has enormous potential to preserve, protect and vastly improve Pennsylvania. Only the state constitution itself has greater power to do good.

It is important to recognize that, save for specific powers granted to the federal government, the state is the sole governmental authority in Pennsylvania. All of Pennsylvania's counties, cities, townships, school districts, and special authorities are mere creatures of the state. They can be reorganized or abolished at will by the state legislature, or by a constitutional amendment initiated by the legislature. The state therefore has vast powers to coordinate the actions of its agencies and local governments for our common good. It cannot do so, however, without a plan.

Pennsylvania could establish a comprehensive plan in two ways:

• It could create a detailed statewide plan, as New Jersey did, that defines specific areas for growth and conservation.

• It could create a series of planning goals, as Maryland and Oregon did, which local municipalities are expected to follow. In Maryland, no state funds may be spent for projects which conflict with the goals. In Oregon, the goals are enforced by a state board of appeals that can reverse or remand local land use decisions.

Although no one can predict what Pennsylvania's plan might contain, I believe that fostering beautiful, efficient, friendly, and conscientious communities would be at the top of the list. The following is my version of a state plan to accomplish that end.

Cornerstones of a state plan

Economic development: Economic growth is best encouraged by clearly demarcating areas where development serves the public good and where it does not. Streamlined permitting procedures shall be established to encourage development in the proper areas.

Cities, villages, and towns: The preponderance of social, historical, and environmental evidence shows that cities, villages and towns are the best living patterns for our citizens, except for those people engaged in farming, forestry, and certain other occupations. Therefore, all Commonwealth agencies and local governments are directed to nurture cities, villages and towns and to discourage sprawling forms of development. The preservation of historic buildings shall be encouraged.

Walking: The preponderance of social and scientific evidence shows that walking is a highly desirable human activity, one that encourages good health and sociability. Therefore, all cities, villages, and towns shall be designed to promote walking.

Equality: A true commonwealth ensures that citizens of all races, ages, classes, and incomes are accorded equal opportunities and protections. To assure these goals are met, the Commonwealth shall expect all communities to provide a mix of housing within the same neighborhoods that people of all incomes can afford.

Tax sharing: At the same time, tax base sharing shall be instituted among local municipalities. At present, dependence on local real estate taxes separates communities into "haves" and "have-nots," and encourages local officials to promote sprawling development. To ensure fairness and discourage sprawl, municipalities will share 15 percent of their tax base in a regional pool that shall be distributed using a formula giving preference to poorer communities.

Equal educational opportunity: All Pennsylvania children have a right to an equal education wherever they live. To help assure equity and reduce local real estate taxes, all school districts shall receive 100 percent of their funding from the Commonwealth, with allocations to be based on an equal sum for each student enrolled.

Community service: Pennsylvania's democratic form of government depends on the virtue, industry, and social responsibility of its citizens. To foster good citizenship, the Commonwealth shall require every student in a public high school or state university to complete at least 60 hours of unpaid community service during non-school hours as a requirement for graduation.

Implementing the plan

A state plan will require Pennsylvania to reallocate its zoning powers. Pennsylvania is different from virtually all other states because it has so many local governments — more than 2,500 cities, townships and boroughs with the authority to regulate land use. This makes growth management more difficult than in New England states, which just have cities and towns, or the South and the West, whose states just have cities and counties. To implement its principles, Pennsylvania's state plan must require a regional approach to planning. The state plan would amend the regulatory powers of our local governments as follows:

County-designated Urban Growth Areas: To foster cities, villages and towns surrounded by open space, all Pennsylvania counties shall be directed to adopt plans that designate urban growth areas. All municipalities within the county shall adopt zoning that conforms to the county plan.

Growth areas shall be large enough to accommodate all predicted development for the next twenty years. They shall be revised every ten years. Proposed development within growth areas will be encouraged by a swift and predictable review process. Development outside the boundaries, except for agriculture and forestry, will be heavily restricted. Water and sewer authorities shall be consolidated and placed under the jurisdiction of the county.

Metropolitan governments: Five regions of Pennsylvania — greater Philadelphia, Pittsburgh, Harrisburg, Scranton-Wilkes-Barre, and Allentown-Bethlehem-Easton — comprise functioning metropolitan areas that extend beyond the boundaries of one county. In accordance with the state plan, the legislature shall establish metropolitan governments in these regions. The governments shall have popularly elected representatives with the power to establish a regional land-use plan, raise revenues, establish urban growth boundaries, operate a consolidated regional water and sewer system, determine the location of all transportation infrastructure, and operate a regional mass transportation system.

Livable communities: Local municipalities shall adopt zoning to encourage walkable communities within urban growth areas. Offices, stores, and schools shall be placed within walking distance of homes.

Greenbelts and greenways: All counties will be encouraged to create a system of greenbelts, permanently protected open space surrounding towns, and greenways, landscaped corridors for walking and riding bicycles, to enhance the urban environment.

Official map: To foster well-planned, contiguous development, local municipalities shall adopt an official map, showing where all streets, greenways, and utility lines will be placed in developing areas. The map must be consistent with the municipal comprehensive plan, zoning ordinance, and capital improvements program.

Brownfields: Vacant, previously developed land will be given top priority for new development. A special real estate transfer tax shall be charged whenever farmland is sold for development, with the proceeds going to remediate and redevelop brownfield sites.

Building rehabilitation: To encourage the reuse of older buildings, local code enforcement officers shall be trained to recognize and implement the "rehab-friendly" provisions of Pennsylvania's Uniform Construction Code.

Affordable housing: Zoning laws shall require communities to contain a mixture of all housing types — small apartment buildings, townhouses, small homes, and large homes — within the same neighborhoods. One of every three dwellings constructed in any given neighborhood shall be affordable to people earning less than the median income for the region.

Coordination of state agencies and local governments: Every state agency — from the Department of Transportation to the Department of Education — shall be required to follow the state plan. All local governments and authorities shall follow the plan.

Urban and community policy: All new state facilities shall be located in cities and boroughs. To encourage a sense of community, all public school employees, including teachers and administrators, will be expected to live in the district that employs them. Local government workers will be expected to live in the municipality that employs them.

Municipal Hearing Board: The state plan shall establish a quasi-judicial Pennsylvania Municipal Board, similar to ones in Oregon and Washington state, that shall rule on all questions relating to the state plan.

Creating a world 'nearer to the heart's desire'

The world has changed enormously since our basic forms of government were established, but human nature has not.

We all need meaningful work, good housing, a sense of security in our neighborhoods, love and friendship, and amicable relations with others. We care most about those who live and work among us, because they have the biggest impact on our lives.

In recent decades, a pattern of life has evolved in Pennsylvania that has turned us inward, isolating us in our houses and our cars instead of encouraging community life. We live in one place and work in another far away. The traditional towns where many residents lived and worked in the same place, where people casually met and socialized on Main Street, where children could be independent, and where citizens basically trusted each other, have largely passed away. But this kind of community can be revived, if we will it so.

Unfortunately, some believe that people of diverse ages and incomes can't get along in one neighborhood. Some find diversity frightening. But as Professor Ray Oldenburg writes in *The Great Good Place:* "Consensus follows interaction and involvement more often than it precedes it. Individuals, like neighborhoods, evolve and develop. When people are thrown together, they discover much to like, to get attached to, to add to their lives, and to change their minds about."

A state plan is nothing more than a way of focusing all the powers of government toward building communities, not dismantling them. It is a way of fostering government that we regard as an association of friends and neighbors, not a "big brother" to be feared and loathed. And we can do this best by creating human scale communities in which we are personally involved.

Theodore Roosevelt coined the term "muck-raker" to describe journalists who could only see the bad. "The men with the muck-rakes are often indispensable to the well-being of society," he said, "but only if they know when to stop raking the muck, and to look upward to the celestial crown of worthy endeavor. There are beautiful things above and roundabout them; and if they gradually grow to feel the whole world is nothing but muck, their power of usefulness is gone."

The media, in their ceaseless search for greater market share, bombard us and our children with hate, violence, fear, and cynicism. We must not be overwhelmed and defeated by it.

It may seem awfully far-fetched to think Pennsylvanians would willingly leave suburbia to live in cities, villages, and towns. Safe, lovely neighborhoods that house residents of all races, ages, and incomes? That, too, seems unachievable.

Now we have the environmental movement. During the last decade, there has been an unprecedented global consensus that nations must reduce their greenhouse gas emissions to prevent catastrophic changes in the climate that will harm every person.

There's nothing we can do that will help our environment more than to live in cities, villages, and towns. I believe Pennsylvanians can be persuaded to do that. After all, few people living a century ago could imagine living anywhere but cities, villages, and towns.

Of all the fifty states and the nations of the world, we in Pennsylvania have a unique heritage. Pennsylvania is a testament to the tremendous power of idealism.

In an age that was just as selfish and cynical as our own, William Penn actually believed it was possible for people of all races and classes and religions to live in peace and harmony and govern themselves according to the Quaker ideals of virtue and love. And while he fell short of that lofty goal, he did establish the most enlightened government of his day, anywhere in the world. His 1682 Frame of Government was a major influence a hundred years later when Washington and Madison and Hamilton came to Philadelphia, the city of brotherly love, to create modern democracy.

I look forward to the day when more people discover how pleasant it is to live in places like my home town of Pottstown, where you can actually walk where you need to go. I look forward to the revival of Philadelphia and our other cities as attractive, even fashionable, places to live, making them once again the focus of our pride.

Just as it took many decades to devastate our cities, it will take many years to reverse the process. But it can be done.

And it's going to happen because of people like you — people who care about the environment and social justice, who want a better life for our children, and who are willing to get involved — the elite group Theodore Roosevelt called "the Fellowship of the Doers."

But great cultural changes have already taken place in our lifetimes. No one — not even the experts — foresaw the amazing changes in Eastern Europe and the former Soviet Union that have transpired in recent years.

Few people believed, back when Martin Luther King began working to integrate the South in 1955, that this civil rights movement would bring about the major culture changes it did, especially as soon as it did.

Pennsylvania's first steps toward a comprehensive plan

There are reasons for hope in Pennsylvania. Two years after this book was first published in 1995, then-Gov. Tom Ridge appointed the 21st Century Environment Commission, a forty-member panel with representatives from business, environmental groups, universities, and state agencies, to recommend ways to improve Pennsylvania's environment in the 21st Century. After a year's study, the panel concluded that sprawling development is the state's No. 1 environmental problem.

In response, Gov. Ridge ordered state agencies to review their policies to find ways to reduce sprawl. Specifically, he ordered the state's Center for Local Government to:

• Submit an annual report on land use trends in Pennsylvania.

• Develop an inventory of sound land use practices.

• Organize a committee of state agencies to review each department's policies to find ways to discourage sprawling development.

• Make recommendations on changes needed in state law and state policy.

By the spring of 2000, the Pennsylvania General Assembly and the governor established two new programs, called "Growing Greener" and "Growing Smarter," to encourage better planning and save open space. "Growing Greener" allocated $650 million over five years to protect watersheds, reclaim mines, and preserve farmland. "Growing Smarter" provided incentives for municipalities to adopt joint comprehensive plans and zoning laws. By late 2003, 187 multi-municipal planning efforts involving 634 municipalities were underway across the state.

A comprehensive study released in December 2003 by the Brookings Institution, funded by Pennsylvania foundations, confirmed that state spending for economic development in recent decades has encouraged growth in the wrong areas, leading to the "hollowing out" of traditional communities.

The study urged Pennsylvania to refocus its spending to reinvest in established cities, towns, and older suburbs, where young, highly educated workers want to live, or it won't be able to compete in the global economy.

Gov. Ed Rendell, whose term began in 2003, has pledged to do that. "The revitalization of Pennsylvania's towns *is* the revitalization of Pennsylvania," he says.

Pennsylvania has a long, long way to go. But we've taken the first few steps, and there's growing optimism that we can, indeed, save our land and save our towns.

Right: Spring comes to Somerset County. Only a state plan can ensure these beautiful farm scenes will endure for future generations.

End page: Five-year-old Jacob Byham enjoys a walk through Meadville's center square in the reassuring company of his grandfather.

What you can do to get involved

The best way to promote cities, villages, and towns, of course, is to live and work in one. You'll find you can lower your cost of living and increase your quality of life at the same time. You can also help bring about positive change by getting involved in the democratic process:

- Educate yourself. Keep up with projects planned in your area. Visit your local municipality to see what kind of planning your community is doing for the future.
- Help spread the word about the need for good planning. Give a copy of this book to your local elected officials, members of local planning commissions, and other influential members of your community.
- Ask your local Cable TV provider to show the public television documentary, *Saving Pennsylvania*, which is based on *Save Our Land, Save Our Towns*. Copies can be obtained from RB Books, Harrisburg. Call 717.232.7944. Cable telecast rights are free.
- Call or write your local elected officials. Attend meetings. Don't be afraid to ask questions. Urge your local government to take an active role in determining the future of your community. Get involved with your local planning board.
- Call or write your county officials to encourage the creation of a countywide comprehensive plan designed to save your towns and countryside. Ask how you can get involved and be supportive.
- Call or write your state legislators and urge them to support measures, such as those listed on pages 122 and 123 of this book, to preserve our towns and countryside.
- Write a letter to the editor of your local newspaper about ways we can discourage sprawling development.
- Look for articles with good ideas for reviving cities, villages and towns. Send copies with a personal note to local officials.
- Join one or more of the following organizations. They may or may not endorse all of the specific ideas in this book, but they are dedicated to saving our land, saving our towns, and helping Pennsylvania live up to its potential.

Scores of civic groups are part of a statewide alliance, called 10,000 Friends of Pennsylvania, to promote progressive land use policies in the Commonwealth.

10,000 Friends of Pennsylvania
117 South 17th Street, Suite 2300
Philadelphia, PA 19103
877.568.2225   www.10000friends.org

Save Our Land, Save Our Towns
222 Chestnut Street
Pottstown, PA 19464
610.323.6837
www.saveourlandsaveourtowns.org

Preservation Pennsylvania
257 North Street
Harrisburg, PA 17101
717.234.2310   www.preservationpa.org

Pennsylvania Environmental Council
117 South 17th Street, Suite 2300
Philadelphia, PA 19103
215.563.0250   www.pecpa.org

Citizens for Pennsylvania's Future
610 N. Third Street
Harrisburg, PA 17101
717.214.7920   www.pennfuture.org

National Trust for Historic Preservation
1785 Massachusetts Avenue NW
Washington, DC 20036
202.588.6000   www.nationaltrust.org

Smart Growth America
1200 18th Street NW, Suite 801
Washington, DC 20036
202-207-3350   www.smartgrowthamerica.org

Sierra Club - Pennsylvania Chapter
600 N. 2nd St., Box 663
Harrisburg, PA 17108-0663
717.232.0101   www.sierraclub.org